What people are saying about…

OVERCOMING
Mediocrity©

5 out of 5 Stars

Incredibly Inspiring!

"This book will make the reader jump off the couch and dive directly into their hopes and dreams. Told from a variety of viewpoints, these women show that anything is possible if one is willing to work hard for their dreams. The reader will be infused with hope and inspiration. I highly recommend reading this book and the rest of the Overcoming Mediocrity series of books from Christie Ruffino."

—Christine

5 out of 5 stars

Extraordinary

"Mediocrity. It's like having a fire in your life that's only smoldering. These women's stories are inspiring, irresistible, and motivating."

—Jack's Mum

5 out of 5 stars

Couldn't Stop Reading… Loved It!

"Pure gold! I would recommend this for anyone who is looking for stories of real people who have overcome challenges. Loved the specific strategies they shared and resources they provided."

—Little

5 out of 5 stars
Inspirational on all New Levels!

"What an amazing book. The power of these women is inspiring! Especially the story from 'Brittany Prince' absolutely amazing, inspiring, and something anyone looking to summon inner strength should read!"

—Robert

5 out of 5 Stars
Very Inspiring!

"It is so great hearing how these women have not stopped in the face of life happening. In these times, this is needed more than ever. A great read for those who are looking to empower other women."

—Lauren

5 out of 5 Stars
Wonderful Motivational Book! So Inspiring!

Wonderful motivational book! Very uplifting stories. I bought a couple for my Christmas and birthday presents!"

—Ericka

5 out of 5 Stars
Highly Recommend!!

"HIGHLY RECOMMEND!!! If you are looking for personal and professional development, this book is for you! It is perfectly inspiring, educational, empowering and beautifully written! I could really relate to the struggles in their personal stories and it has helped me to continue working on overcoming my own obstacles so I can succeed in life and in business! Thank you all for sharing your incredible journeys."

—Lisa

5 out of 5 Stars

Excellent Read for Men and Women!

"LOVED THE BOOK! [Husband] thought it should not be limited to a "women's" book — excellent for men and women. Writing was personal, intimate, yet clearly educational in nature. Long enough to take you somewhere, but short enough to sit down and read right then. The book is downloaded on our Kindle, so we can read again."

—TJ

5 out of 5 Stars

Very Inspiring!

"Thank you, ladies, for telling your stories. So inspiring, love the book. Bought multiple copies to give to my girlfriends that are unstoppable woman in my life. Thank you."

—Julie

5 out of 5 Stars

Uplifting and Inspirational!

"Very inspiring, powerful book! Love women supporting women! Would highly recommend!"

—Amazon Reviewer

5 out of 5 Stars

Fearlessly and Wonderfully Made!

"This book is so encouraging and uplifting I couldn't put it down. I originally got this book to support one of my dear friends but quickly fell in love with every story that I read. The encouragement that came from every story hit in every aspect of my life. I'm so grateful something like this was written. The younger generation definitely needs to hear stories and successful stories of women that suffer through some hard times and come out victorious!!"

—Eden

5 out of 5 Stars

It's a Great Investment in Yourself!

"This is an inspiring compilation. Each woman's story contains powerful lessons that are widely applicable. Heartwarming and triumphant all at the same time. Any woman who's tread a rocky path on her life's journey will be able to relate and rejoice along with each author as she overcomes adversity and challenge. If you're seeking inspiration to overcome adversity, take a moment to breathe, regroup, and soak up a story or three. It's a great investment in yourself."

—Debbra

What our clients are saying about…

OVERCOMING
Mediocrity©

"If you're on the fence, I'd highly recommend and encourage you to jump in feet first because not only did I get to work with other amazing women, but I also ended up being an Amazon Bestselling Author which is a huge boost for my career and brand. I hope that you'll choose to share your inspiring story for all of the many women who are going to read it."

—Amber Champagne-Matos
Founder of Champagne Apothecary
Overcoming Mediocrity Unstoppable Women

"I'm passionate about helping women overcome the lies that are holding them back. The problem was that I still believed my own lies. I questioned if my story could actually make a difference, feared that no one would want to hear it and didn't trust I could write it well enough for it to be published. Until I met Christie. She invited me to share my story in one of her books, and it completely transformed my business, my life and best of all, the lives of the women who read it. They've reached out to me, grateful for how what I shared helped them overcome their adversities. Hearing those women's testimonies gave me confidence and fueled me to keep writing. With Christie's help, I published my own book just a few months later, and am currently writing the next in that series."

—Shannon Ferraby
Author, Speaker & Trainer with Success Unwrapped
Overcoming Mediocrity Influential Women

"*Being a part of this book made such a difference and I love the conversations that Christie and I had together. They were so rich and revealing that I actually can do a TED talk. But really, what really broke through for me is being able to share my story and to be a subject expert. Since then, I've been on other people's podcasts and I started my own podcast 'Tea Time Midlife Edition.' If you have a story that you want to share with the world, get in front of Christie.*"

—Regina Young
Podcaster and CEO of Modelperfect Woman
Overcoming Mediocrity Unstoppable Women

"*Being an Amazon Bestselling Author alongside some fabulous women in this series has propelled me forward in ways that I wouldn't have had otherwise. I've since guested on podcasts, I have an episode on Amazon Fire TV, and I've had so many women tell me how inspired they've been by the book. Secondarily, I was able to tell my story in a really authentic way and not have it completely rearranged in the editing process. I'm really excited to see what the future holds.*"

—Tiffany Lewis
CEO of More Meaningful Marketing
Overcoming Mediocrity Unstoppable Women

"*Christie Ruffino is a master at taking women's women who are passionate about telling their story, but they don't know exactly how they're going to do it and molding us into not only authors but Amazon Bestselling Authors. It was an amazing six-month journey, where I got to meet some amazing women, discover their stories, and realize that what I have to say is important and something that the world needs to hear.*"

—Danica Joan
Founder of Kids Need Both, Inc
Overcoming Mediocrity Unstoppable Women

"Me, an Amazon number one Bestselling Author. What a crazy exciting journey this has been and an accomplishment I would have never dreamed of. Joining the Overcoming Mediocrity project has brought me so many new connections, as well as the credibility and the credentials for my business. Becoming an author is something I never planned to do in my lifetime but has been a very, very exciting ride!"

—Laura Fank-Carrara
President of Laura Ocean Solutions
Overcoming Mediocrity Unstoppable Women

"Being an author in the series has opened doors for me. It makes it easier to rise to the top of the list for those responsible for booking speaking gigs to want to talk to me. The traffic to my website and Business Page has increased measurably. It has shortened the know, like, trust factor. People are reaching out to me first before I reach out to them. The titles of the books help women who want to stretch themselves. Who wouldn't want to associate themselves and work with an author who is Dynamic, Resilient, Strong, and Influential?"

—Jeanne Lyons
Career Breakthrough Coach
Overcoming Mediocrity Influential Women

"Christie and the OM team took an overwhelming and complicated process of book publishing and made it very easy to get my story published. I was guided through the process from start to finish. Every detail was outlined, and my questions were always answered promptly. The book has received rave reviews, and it has taken my credibility to the next level, as I am now an Amazon #1 best seller! Thank you!!"

—Lynn O'Dowd
Motivational Speaker and Keynote Performer
Overcoming Mediocrity Influential Women

"When I learned about this project, I was already fully into the writing, publishing, and marketing process of my other book, Getting Yourself Unstuck. However, I couldn't put everything in that book. Therefore, Overcoming Mediocrity allowed me to publish a very personal story that didn't seem to fit in my other book. Now going forward in my marketing, the two books will work in tandem."

—Angie Engstrom
Coach and Plank Trainer
Overcoming Mediocrity Resilient Women

"Christie and her team made the process of becoming an Amazon Bestselling Author easy and fun. There are resources and support every step of the way, and now I have a book to grow my business."

—Amanda Tobinski
Magnetic Media Group
Overcoming Mediocrity Fearless Women

OVERCOMING MEDIOCRITY

Other Overcoming Mediocrity Titles

Overcoming Mediocrity — Dynamic Women

Overcoming Mediocrity — Courageous Women

Overcoming Mediocrity — Strong Women

Overcoming Mediocrity — Remarkable Women

Overcoming Mediocrity — Resilient Women

Overcoming Mediocrity — Influential Women

Overcoming Mediocrity — Victorious Women

Overcoming Mediocrity — Fearless Women

Overcoming Mediocrity — Unstoppable Women

Overcoming Mediocrity — Empowered Women

LIMITLESS WOMEN

OVERCOMING

Mediocrity ©

**A unique collection of stories from limitless women
who have created their own lives of significance!**

Presented by Christie Lee Ruffino

DPWN Publishing

www.OvercomingMediocrity.org

This book is a compilation of stories from numerous experts who have each contributed a chapter. It is designed to provide information and inspiration to our readers.

It is sold with the understanding that the publisher and the individual authors are not engaged in the rendering of psychological, legal, accounting, or other professional advice. The content and views in each chapter are the sole expression and opinion of its author and not necessarily the views of DPWN Publishing, Christie Lee Ruffino, or the Dynamic Professional Women's Network, Inc.

For more information, contact:
DPWN Publishing
A division of the Dynamic Professional Women's Network, Inc.
1879 N. Neltnor Blvd. #316, West Chicago, IL 60185
www.OvercomingMediocrity.org
www.OurDPWN.com

Printed in the United States of America

ISBN: 978-1-939794-25-3

Dedication

This book is dedicated to the twenty limitless women whose stories are in this book and the countless women who bravely navigated through every twist and turn during this unprecedented time in human history: the COVID-19 epidemic.

A special dedication to the most LIMITLESS woman in my life, Jesica Nicole Ruffino. Jesica continually faces challenges in her life with strength, confidence, grace, and a few choice words now and then. She is a brilliant, caring, and supportive daughter and a fun, fabulous, and loving mom to the two most adorable children ever. (And I have thousands of photos to prove it.) I love you to the moon and beyond! XXOO

The Power of a Story

There is nothing more important in this world than the relationships we build and the legacy we leave in the lives of those who've crossed paths with us on our journey of life. It's the experiences we have during this journey that define our individual uniqueness and create our own powerful personal blueprint or our unique story snowflake.

It is this blueprint that can empower and equip us to possess a distinct advantage over every other person in this world, if leveraged correctly and shared. If we don't have the courage to share our snowflake, it will be lost forever. No one will have the same story, and no one can repeat your story. Therefore, those who come after you will never learn anything from what you've experienced and what you've learned if you don't share it.

I feel that the most significant thing we can do to add value back to this world, is to master the narrative of our lives. All of our leadership and moneymaking abilities rest in our ability to discover, craft, and deliver our personal story or message in a way that will allow people to connect to us. The right story shared at the right time with the right person can alter the trajectory of their life, as well as our own.

I have also discovered, how therapeutic the process of owning our story is for us to become ready and empowered to write the next chapter of our life journey. I have seen women from our books bravely face their past, discover their true purpose, reclaim the power that had diminished over the years, and pivot onto an exciting new path. They launch a new business, up-level their existing business, or they ease into retirement with a renewed passion and fervor for life.

Embracing our story will change the direction of our next story and unveil our ultimate destiny.

Power to you and the story of your life!

"When you can own your story and step into a business that is aligned with your gifts, strengths, and passions to serve, then the right people, resources, and opportunities will come to you at the right time because the reason is right."

—Christie Lee Ruffino

Introduction

When I embarked upon this journey, never in my wildest dreams did I expect it to turn out as it has. My motives were grand, yet much more simplistic than they are today.

My initial goal was to create one co-authored book, collecting stories from women I admired who were members of my organization, the Dynamic Professional Women's Network (DPWN). I knew how sharing my story in a similar book (compiled by a mentor of mine, Michelle Prince) had been transformational for me. I also knew how having a book to share in the business community gave me additional credibility, recognition, and exposure. What I didn't know was how these same stories would be just as transformational for the readers, as they related with one or more of the women who were willing to share their stories in such a vulnerable and authentic way.

I also had no way of knowing how working with these women would lead me down a path that would change "my" life forever…

My Story

I'm a natural connector. Many women are. I believe it's part of our DNA to connect people with other people or resources that can help them. I've often shared how my journey to build DPWN was not intentional. As an introvert, the last thing I wanted to do was build a business where I would have to frequently talk with new people… strangers. But thankfully, God knew better than I did what was best for me.

Now, 19 years later, our community has had to evolve since in-person networking has ceased in many areas due to the pandemic. We pivoted like so many other businesses. We tried a few things that worked and tried a few things that didn't work. We added more global members, supported the members who lost their businesses, and we continue to celebrate the local chapters that remained loyally dedicated to each other at a time when they needed each other the most. At this time, we are anxiously anticipating the day when ALL of our chapters can resume meeting again at local business locations, we can begin launching new chapters in new areas, and we can continue to expand our network benefits. You can connect with us at www.OurDPWN.com.

I personally work with women to help them identify their signature story and build a profitable, purpose-driven business helping others. That is my passion and where my story has brought me thus far. I'm blessed to wake up every day, knowing that I can help my clients step into their next story. We are all creating a wonderful butterfly effect. You can connect with me at www.ChristieRuffino.com.

Our *Overcoming Mediocrity Project* is going just as strong, celebrating book number eleven featuring an amazing lineup of limitless women, our second podcast year, a brand-new online gift summit, and an upcoming retreat. The stories from each of our women are about strength, faith, and courage. They are about having the confidence to believe in ourselves, even when those we love may not. They are about having the courage to do hard things, even when we don't want to. And, they are about having a limitless mindset through all of life's ups and downs because that is what, as women, we do brilliantly.

Do you have a story of strength, faith, or courage? You can connect with us at www.OvercomingMediocrity.org.

Your Story

What is your story?

Are you living your story, or are you living for someone else's story? Maybe you are living into your destiny. Or maybe you spend the majority of your time unhappily working for someone else, taking care of someone else, or doing something that does not create a fire in your soul. You're managing. However, you just can't seem to escape those pesty thought bubbles popping into your mind, reminding you that… "One of these days, it will be MY TURN."

What if that time never comes?

The personal and professional development industry generates billions of dollars of revenue every year. According to www.marketresearch.com, the U.S. estimated market value for personal coaching was $955 million in 2015. In 2019 the estimated market value was $2.849 billion. That's a 21% increase over the 2015 estimate. The coaching industry remains strong, and, despite the economic downturn due to COVID-19, the industry will reach $20 billion by 2022. The great news is that for every one of those coaches, there are countless people desperately searching for help.

I work with women who have reached a point in their lives, where they're finally ready to step into their destiny, own their story, and share their wisdom. Women who don't think they have the skills to become a coach, but they know down deep in their gut that they CAN help people. They're considering stepping into a coaching or consulting role, but they don't know where to start. Or they've been trying, and they're just not getting the results they desire (or frankly that they deserve).

If you just read that and felt a butterfly or two swirling around in your stomach, then maybe we should chat. I have a simple system that will provide you with the steps and support to build a profitable business as a coach, author, and speaker.

Our Books — Their Story

Our first *Overcoming Mediocrity* book was a smashing success! On the very first day of its release in 2013, it became the #1 downloaded Kindle book in the motivational genre category. Twenty-two women shared their stories to inspire other women to overcome and succeed as they had, and all authors were able to claim the distinguished Amazon Bestselling Author status.

Because of the overwhelming success of that first book, we went on to produce additional books under the *Overcoming Mediocrity* brand. Each of them also climbed to the #1 position on Amazon on the very first day of release. Four of them, *Overcoming Mediocrity — Resilient Women, Influential Women, Fearless Women,* and *Empowered Women,* all reached the #1 position in two categories which was a great accomplishment.

These books have ultimately taken on a life of their own and have made a greater impact than ever anticipated. It is exciting to read testimonials from women who have read and connected with one or more of the inspirational stories inside. It's even more exciting when one of those same women decide to share their story in one of our future books.

It is now with great honor and pride that I can share stories from the limitless women in this book. I've had the pleasure of getting to know each of these ladies and learning about the stories they're sharing with you. I'm deeply inspired by the courage they're exhibiting. They are sharing the personal details of their lives with the sole intention of allowing you, the reader, to learn from their experiences and wisdom.

It's easy to become complacent. Live a life of mediocrity, just coasting through day by day. It takes courage to fight through the hard and overcome challenges that seem impossible to defeat. The women in the pages of this book made a purposeful choice to live significant lives and share their stories to help you also live a life of significance. This demonstrates strength, humility, and the heart of a true go-giver. These women all have even greater things yet to come. They are women whom you should know, learn from, and emulate.

This book is meant to not only encourage you but to also awaken your inner desire to share your story along with them. Each woman in our project wants to make the biggest possible impact in the world and transform as many lives as possible, by sharing their story and wisdom in a book that will get massive exposure. They could have kept their stories private. That would have been the safest and easiest path for them. However, they decided to step out of their comfort zone and share the narratives of their lives with you. We invite you to join them on this journey.

I am blessed to have the opportunity to share these LIMITLESS women with you. I hope you feel just as blessed to receive the value they offer you.

Hugs & Blessings,

Christie

Table of Contents

Christine Alt Parry

You Are Either in, or You Are Out

I was always a driven person. I knew how to create a punch list and check off all the boxes. Here are some examples:

- I owned a company called "Art 2 Wear" in the early 1990s, with national accounts.

- I graduated with honors from Northwestern University in 1994.

- I had a marketing and PR business in Chicago for five years.

- I made a living in an industry fraught with rejection — modeling and acting — and paid the bills with it for 20 years.

- I was (and still am) a successful real estate investor with multiple rental properties.

- I had a dream job selling stuff on live television at the largest shopping channel in the world — QVC.

- I have written three books and illustrated a fourth.

I was really good at getting what I wanted because reinventing myself has always been a way of life for me. These days, people call it agility. For me, it was survival. I have also sold wine and spirits, worked as an automotive product specialist, marketing director, PR manager, project manager, artist, model, actress, voiceover artist, coach, and executive trainer. When people would ask me what my passion was, my pat reply was, "Variety!" I fancied myself as being limitless. However, the truth was, I was at war against my own internal limitations. It was never "enough." I was always constantly striving for something bigger, better, and brighter. I grew up without a father and had some serious issues with commitment. I had been engaged three times but had never married. My excuse was that I worked weird hours, and most of the men I would meet couldn't stomach my erratic schedule. I always felt something was missing without having a soul mate in my life, and struggled with loneliness for several years.

So here I finally was, on the beautiful pink sand beaches in Elbow Beach, Bermuda, looking my beloved fiancé in the eyes, as I said I do at 41 years of age. Yes, my ship had finally come in, and I was marrying Mr. Right. God had finally blessed me with the one I had hoped for. David was (and is) handsome, funny, kind, and shares many of my Christian beliefs. He owned a large plumbing contracting business specializing in new construction, was an inventor with two successful products, and is a published author. As for me, I had built up a tidy sum in stocks and real estate investments, and I was willing to share it. I was finally ready for my next vocation as wife to this wonderful man. I was marrying someone who I truly loved, and I was really happy. The potential seemed, well, limitless.

It rained heavily on our wedding day, which some say is an omen for a rough and rocky marriage. However, I wasn't about to buy into an old wives' tale. We exchanged our vows barefoot on the beautiful pink sand and scampered into the tide with abandon. Since we had eloped, there was no one else in attendance, save a Scottish minister in full regalia despite the 90° temperatures. David was divorced and had four children. I admit that I really had no idea what I was getting into at first, marrying a man with four kids. I never wanted them to think I was trying to be their mother, but rather, their friend. We did agree to sign a prenuptial agreement before getting married. I wanted David to feel confident that I would not go after his business, if our relationship didn't work out. Friends from church suggested marital counseling, as they were concerned about our welfare. I had been through therapy before and was open to it. The counselor was empathetic and approved of the union.

At first, I thought I had died and gone to heaven. I no longer had to work because David covered all of the bills. We had the kids on the weekends, since that was the way it had been set up after his divorce. My loneliness suddenly evaporated. I was able to continue my dream to go on air as a regularly scheduled guest expert at QVC and landed a plum contract as a spokesperson for Kodak cameras. I picked up additional work as a product specialist at auto shows and special events on weekends. This was my attempt at compromise. I was giving the kids alone time with David while I traveled.

Six months later, two of David's children came to live with us full-time. This was not what I had planned on, and all of us were unhappy. I didn't think I'd be able to remain in our current residence, 1700 square feet, with two teenage boys, so we decided to build the house of our dreams. I sold my rental properties in Chicago, and we used the cash as a down payment to begin building a 7,500 square-foot home. David leveraged lines of credit against his business to make his contribution to the effort. This did not help matters because he was already financially extended after his divorce. Still, this was 2008. It was a great time to be in construction. Real estate was priced through the roof, the new housing boom was skyrocketing, and David's work seemed like it would never dry up. We just figured if we could get through the next couple of years, we would be fine.

Suddenly the housing bubble burst and new construction came to an abrupt halt. The value of housing dropped 50 percent. Lehman Brothers went out of business, which then caused the stock market to take a dramatic fall. All my prized investments that I had strategically selected were worth half of what they were when I bought them. While I looked like a genius selling my rentals right before the crash, that money was now wrapped up in our dream home, which was turning into a nightmare. I no longer had rental income, but I was fortunate to have both QVC and my GMC contracts.

By 2010, David was officially declared bankrupt. The only thing that kept us from being thrown out on the street was the prenuptial agreement that

I had signed, keeping my own financial assets intact. We sold our dream home ten days before the bank was to foreclose on it. Thankfully, we were able to pay off the bank and take back my down payment. However, we needed a new place to live, so I was forced to sell my stock portfolio at a 50% loss because I could not get financing due to David's bankruptcy. With this, we bought a much smaller home with cash. To say I was bitter and angry was an understatement. I was always the shrewd one, or so I had thought. Instead, I felt like I made the mother of all huge mistakes that I would have to live with for many years to come.

It was during this time that I started thinking that maybe this marriage was not for me. I started losing desire for my husband because I did not respect him anymore. Yet when it was time to move into our new house, something in me would not let me sever our connection. I felt like God had other plans for us. Therefore, we continued to live together physically, while emotionally and mentally, we were rapidly moving miles apart from one another. Soon after, Kodak discontinued its digital camera division, and QVC came to an end for me. David was trying to figure out what he wanted to do next with his life. I got him involved in special events and auto shows, and he began working regularly in Chicago, Las Vegas, and California as an automotive expert. He was really good at it because he has a way with people and is terrific in sales. Rather than being happy that David was working, I was fixated on what I had wanted, which was that entrepreneurial guy I had dreamed about. I had always vowed I would never marry someone who did what I did for a living, yet here I was, staring a perceived limitation squarely in the eye. I had always wanted to be married to a guy who was successful, so I could be proud of him. The trouble was, I was viewing David as an extension of myself. As much as I tried to trust God through this whole process, I felt like He had let me down. I felt like I had to wait and be single all this time, only to regret the fact that I hadn't married for money like I had originally intended to when I was younger. To say I had a bad attitude was an understatement.

In 2013, I left the freelance world out of necessity and took a full-time contract position with a large automotive manufacturer. I was hired to be a training facilitator of learning for their broad array of products. This required more than just standing up and delivering a presentation, like I was accustomed to at the auto show. I needed to coach my students on how to assimilate product knowledge and make it uniquely their own through sales pitches they would ultimately deliver to their customers. I began with features and benefits walk-around presentations. Talking about a feature and explaining how it would benefit a customer was similar to what I did at QVC. It came naturally to me, and I enjoyed it. One of the best things about the job is that it forced me to get out of my own head and remain positive, even in the face of sheer terror (I was afraid the sales consultants at the dealerships would figure out that I had no idea what I was actually doing). I also needed to maintain a good attitude in front of my students, which carried over into my personal life. The job also meant a steady paycheck. I truly hoped the consistency of it all would translate into a happier home life. The hard part was that my husband was not working as much as I was, due to the sporadic nature of the freelance world. I became resentful that working full-time was no longer an option for me but a necessity.

David then took a job power washing homes. This, to me, seemed to reach an all-new low. I completely lost whatever modicum of respect I had for my husband. I decided I didn't want to be married to him anymore. I went to an attorney and asked her what it would take to dissolve the marriage. She assured me it would be easy and for me to just let her know when I wanted to proceed. Something in my heart still wouldn't let me do it, so I blamed it on God and put it off. I spent a lot of time mourning losses and complaining. I had not yet come to the realization that when we complain, we remain.

In 2016, my great friend Vicki Parker mentioned that I should make a decision about David. She told me that I needed to either be in the relationship or out of it. Anything in the middle was just wasting time and energy. I decided I was finally ready to end it. However, before I went back to the attorney, I enrolled in a weekend-long Landmark Forum Advanced course with the express purpose of trying to figure out how I was going to live my life without

David being a part of it. I was hoping a breakthrough would occur as a result of taking this class.

The Landmark coursework is all about reprogramming patterns and thoughts that we create in our minds, based upon our own experience. These become custom-made "stories" starring us as the protagonist. We tell ourselves these stories so many times that we think they're the truth when, in reality, they're just our interpretation of what actually did happen. If a person wants a different result, they can examine how and why a thing occurs in their lives and tell themselves a different story. I wanted things to occur differently in my life, and I was willing to try anything.

The amazing Larry Pearson was our facilitator for the weekend. I found out later that he had replaced another trainer at the last minute. I have often wondered what would've happened had he not been our facilitator. He focused in on me for some weird reason. It is like he knew his job was to help me save my marriage, even though I was hell-bent on moving on. He challenged me on all the stories I had been telling myself about all these bad things happening to me. He made me face the fact that I had been an active participant in spending money that neither of us could afford and not working harder to maintain decent relationships with David's children. It was time to start telling myself a new story about David and me that was filled with hope and a future together. One of my "homework assignments" was for me to call the kids and make it right. So, I did and apologized for the fact that I hadn't been the person that they had hoped for when I married their dad. I told them that I knew I had let them down and that I was sorry. It was incredibly healing because each of them responded to me so positively. I half expected them to hang up on me!

I left that weekend with a different outlook. I decided I wanted to remain in my marriage. I knew the first thing I had to do was try to get the respect back that I had lost for my husband. I stopped blaming him for everything that had gone wrong and accepted my part in it. I stopped comparing myself to my friends who had married men with great jobs and done it right. Instead, I focused on all the things that had compelled me to marry my husband. I started thinking about all the things I liked about David. I would look at his pretty blue eyes and his beautiful smile and enjoy his great sense of humor. Rather than focus on the lousy power washing job he had to work to pay the electric bill, I would consider the fact that he wanted to pay the electric bill in the first place. I would tell him I was proud of him, even though I didn't feel that way at first. I created a list of things that I loved about him and put it somewhere I could see it. When I felt disappointed, I would look to the list as a reminder.

I removed the limitations I had placed about our relationship in my own mind. When my mind began to drift into the negative, I corrected the thought pattern by telling myself new stories about how I wanted our life together to be. I created a visualization board with pictures of happy couples, a beautiful stone home with a pool in the back, and expensive sports cars. I added pictures of rental properties because I wanted to get back into it eventually. I put the vision board where I could see it, in my office. I hoped that this vision board would become our reality.

I soon picked up a side gig as a process trainer, along with my full-time work. Process training is different than product training, in that it's all about coaching people to create better outcomes for themselves. I really liked it and wanted to learn more. I had spent so much time coaching myself into a better mindset. I felt like I was doing it already. A friend was taking courses at The Institute for Professional Excellence in Coaching (iPEC). I watched her blossom from someone who sort of sat on the sidelines into the kind of woman who commanded attention and shifted the energy in the room around her. She seemed limitless in her approach to life. I decided I wanted some of whatever it was she had, so I signed up for classes in 2019. I was given the tools to overcome the limitations of my past and actively create the new life of my dreams. I was shown how to literally shift the energy in my own life from catabolic (negative) to anabolic (positive). It's sort of like someone gave me a remote control into the television set that is my brain. I was given the power and authority to change the channel to a reality that I wanted. I chose confidence, faith in God, joy, kindness, a happy marriage, great friendships, and a successful career. I also learned how to harness the anabolic energy around me and use it to make myself feel great through encouraging others. Through that, I felt limitless, which gave me more energy. With the change in my attitude and toward what could be, I was able to reignite my affection for my husband and enjoy him for who he is, not what I thought he should be.

A year later, I became a Certified Professional Coach through the International Coaching Foundation (ICF). I also received my Associate Certified Coaching (ACC) credential after completing 100 hours of individual and group coaching. I also received my ELI-MP and am certified as an Energy Leadership Master Practitioner. I now coach many people through my work, and together we co-create sustainable outcomes for their lives. I truly feel that coaching was the piece that was missing post-therapy. I think everyone should experience coaching because it truly changed my life for the better. My life is now filled with limitless possibilities.

Interestingly, I kept that visualization board hidden in my closet all along. It occurred to me that we should go back to our old church, so we started attending regularly. David was then offered a job as a salesman for a car dealership that was owned by friends we knew from that same church. That turned out to be the way he reinvented himself. David put in the time, and within a year he was the number one guy at the dealership, selling up to 30 cars per month. I was eventually able to invest in rental properties near our home. We befriended married couples who were kind and supported us. We renovated our house, and I made sure there was stone on the side of it and on the chimney, just like I had on my visualization board. In due time, I became very proud of David. I realized that through this process, I had also checked off another box: a successful marriage with my wonderful husband!

How was I able to regain the respect back for my husband? Here are some tips that I hope you will consider using, if you are in the same situation that I was.

Act as if. If you want a new result, approach the situation as if the result is already in hand. I wanted my respect back for my husband, so I made a choice to respect him, even though I did not feel that way at first. There's a lot of truth in the old adage, "Fake it, until you make it." Eventually, you will get there.

Forgive the past. No matter what it is, you can't change what happened. Forgiveness is for you, the forgiver, not the person being forgiven. An analogy to it is this: "You Can't Unring the Bell." Try doing that, and you'll see what I mean. Let it go.

Spend more time focusing in what you do want, and less on what you don't want. Try to create a mental image of what you want, and then think about it often. I am a big believer in prayer and meditation.

A story is just that, a story. Don't get stuck in old negative stories that you've been telling yourself for years. See them instead for what they are. Tell yourself a new story of how you want your life to be. Be an active participant in writing the book of your life.

A limiting belief is something someone else told you that they believe is true, and now you do, too. It is not necessarily the actual truth. You can choose to believe something new, if the current belief doesn't work for you. Choose beliefs that resonate from within and uplift you, rather than those that beat you down. Be limitless in your thinking.

Don't assume that just because something happened in a certain way in the past that it's going to occur that way again. Time and chance happen to us all.

God gives everyone who comes to Planet Earth two things: 24 hours in a day and the power of choice. If you can make a different choice, you will experience a different result. Choose wisely!

Christine Alt Parry

Christine was a television personality from 2002 to 2013, appearing on QVC as a regular on-air guest host. She has been in several commercials, infomercials, and industrial films cast in a variety of roles. She has been interviewed in The New York Times, The Milwaukee Sentinel, The Daily Herald, Chicago, and Cosmopolitan magazines as a product expert in technology and automotive. She holds a BA in Marketing from Northwestern University's School of Speech. Christine is an Energy Leadership Master Practitioner and Certified Professional Coach. In 2021, she received her Associate Certified Coach certification from the International Coaching Foundation. Christine is also a member in good standing with the National Speakers Organization.

Christine owned a marketing and PR company in Chicago for several years. She was always intrigued with HR. She partnered with a boutique motivational organization as a customer experience facilitator, encouraging automotive dealership staff to develop transparent relationships with their customers using a series of assessment tools and coaching techniques. Christine now facilitates product and process training as a contractor for Nissan Dealerships in the Northeast. She also works as a transitional coach with select clients in key leadership roles. Christine promotes the idea of great customer experience being the pathway to success in sales.

Christine is the published author of two books: "Memoirs of a Shopping Channel Guest Expert" (Parry, Amazon, 2020) and "Finding Daddy, Finding Me" (Parry, Amazon, Publications International, 2010). She illustrated the Christian Apologetics mini-book, "Santa Claus, the Easter Bunny, the Tooth Fairy, and Jesus," in 2007.

Christine owned Art 2 Wear in the early 1990s, featuring her own hand-painted denim items. She has traveled extensively and visited 71 countries. She lives with her husband, David Parry, and their beloved Mainecoon cats, Dusty, Sasha, and Jasmine, in Exton, Pennsylvania.

Christine Alt Parry
Be The Change You Wish to See, Inc.
Pennsylvania
443-910-3811
facparry@gmail.com
www.ChristineAltParry.com

Christine's 5 Cs of Coaching

- Christine provides Coaching to help remove internal resistance so Clients can achieve sustainable results using their own Conscious decision-making process.

- Co-creation is a process in which we do the work together to co-create a new, more desirable outcome for the Client.

- Coaching involves a Systematic process of asking the right questions and using the Client's answers to discover they had the answers within all along.

- Freed to move forward, the Client is Coached into action to achieve what they want.

For more information, visit www.ChristineAltParry.com or scan the QR Code below.

Felecia Etienne

Own the Struggle...

I thought I was the original badass until I found myself lying in a hospital bed with my feet in the air, paralyzed, terrified with fear, my heart racing, exposed to 8 strangers I had never met before, all alone and not knowing if I would EVER see my family again.

A swarm of doctors and nurses surrounded me, all frantically working to figure out what was wrong. They were probing, scanning, and examining. I felt like I was on quicksand and sinking deeper and deeper, finding it harder and harder to breathe. The one solace was their eyes. I fixated on one nurse's eyes. It was filled with hope.

I was thinking to myself, how did I get here? IT WAS NOT SUPPOSED TO BE THIS WAY...

Less than one hour earlier, I had been standing before an audience at an off-site sales meeting with a group of newly hired VPs. I was teaching them our sales methodologies. What no one knew was that morning, I had woken up feeling a little off. Nothing outside of the norm, but something didn't feel right.

I heard a faint voice whisper. You know that voice. It said, "Something isn't right." It was drowned out by that other voice that said, "Just keep going. You can't afford NOT to show up. You don't get that privilege. You can't disappoint. You can't drop the ball." I pulled myself together, but mid-way during that presentation, that slight feeling of discomfort came roaring back as a sharp pain.

I smiled and pushed my way through it. You know how we do. We listen to our inner voice telling us to "Push Through."

I did everything I needed to do to show up as the badass I thought I was. I ended the presentation with a standing ovation. I aced the dang thing. I even answered questions while feeling the pain. I did what I've learned to do in my life — just pushed through.

I was focused on being of value to the organization, but I didn't see my own worth.

The faint whisper did not subside; it told me, "You have a flight to catch tomorrow morning... Just go and check it out NOW..." What was once a whisper was NOW A YELL... This time I listened... that same voice told me to research the hospitals in the area that could support it if it came down to an emergency.

I listened to that voice, and that voice saved my life...

We all have that voice. She is the voice that pushes you to take that uncomfortable ACTION that gets you to your next level. She is that voice that sees the danger before you see it. She is the voice you hush and push in the corner. That day she said, "NO MORE."

I took an uncomfortable action. I told my colleague that everything was not OK. I remember my colleague frantically trying to figure out what hospitals were in the area and how we could get there. The city was strange; it was our first time traveling there. In a calm voice, I said I had already researched it. I was still in the mode of trying to do everything and protect everyone's feelings because the last thing I wanted was to feel like a burden.

The Shifting Tide

Moments before the doctor cleared me to travel out of Dallas back to NYC, that same faint voice told me to get up and move. I listened and what happened next changed my life forever. Just when I thought everything was going to be OK.

Suddenly, I found being in that room unbearable; the noise was intolerable — so many voices… so many decisions. Two lives were on the line, and both of them precious.

Everyone has an opinion. One opinion I heard a lot was, "Don't be Selfish." My thoughts were racing through my mind. I was struggling to keep composure. Whose life is more valuable? That was the question.

How Did I Get Here?

I tried to do everything for everyone else and didn't take care of myself. I put everyone's needs ahead of my own, but now I was asking myself whether it was all worth it…

Because I realized this might be the end.

The doctors and nurses shared with me that there was nothing more they could do at this point.

I thought: "I'm going into preterm labor, and there's no way to stop it. I'm only 22 weeks pregnant. It's not supposed to be this way."

The debate continued. The consensus was the selfless thing to do, is to do nothing. The best-case scenario is not to resuscitate and try to save your life and not the baby. A fetus is considered viable with a chance of surviving at 24 weeks. I was told not to feel guilty because pregnancies still could be terminated at this point… but all I felt was guilt; the guilt was erupting in my mind… I felt guilty for traveling, for not getting to hug my two kids before I left for the airport, for not listening to my body, for loving my job.

I remember asking questions… and requesting to speak to various specialists. They even rushed a specialist in from NICU while I was being rolled into emergency surgery… The specialist confirmed that, most likely, this baby would be born blind and crippled, with no quality of life. The sanest and most humane thing to do was not to resuscitate. I remember looking into her eyes and seeing the conviction that she genuinely didn't see a positive ending.

Do you want us to resuscitate? Do you want us to try to save the baby?

The most humane thing to do, the most unselfish thing, is to allow us not to try and save the baby, but we need your permission to do that.

Just at that moment, I knew that I had to make this critical decision all alone in pure terror. I desperately wished my husband was with me, but he was many, many miles away. I reflected on my last appointment. It was my anatomy scan. It was a full fetus ultrasound, and everything was perfect. I got the all-clear to travel. The baby was doing great. I was so happy.

Just as I was thinking this, my baby moved inside me. I could still feel the movement even with my body's trauma. I knew this baby was strong.

I made the only decision I could make. Do everything you can to save the baby!

I woke up disoriented by the bright lights in the recovery room. I was alive, but I did not know if my baby had survived. I was surrounded by all the moms holding their precious babies.

The Road Traveled...

My life has never been easy; I learned to be strong and never let them see you sweat. I was raised by two loving parents that wanted the best for me. They raised my two sisters and me very strictly. I remember the love that flowed and the requirements needed to be loved. I learned that I needed always to prove myself because I was already behind because of who I am. I had to work harder, learn more, do more just to be seen. This belief carried me through my life. I'd lay in bed, dreaming of what life would be like when I left and had the freedom to do what I wanted to do. I would visualize being in New York City and committed to getting there no matter what.

I decided the best way to get there was to go away to college. This wasn't welcomed. Based on my parents' strict religious beliefs, they believed that college wasn't a path that should be explored. I didn't know how but knew the why. I applied to schools in New York. I was hit with challenges because I was applying from outside the continental US. I was born and raised on a beautiful Island, but that brought its own sub-culture and limiting beliefs.

I took the uncomfortable action of letting my parents know I'd been accepted to a college, and I was going. They weren't happy but, in the end, they supported me. I got on the plane, holding close to my heart my dreams.

My bubble quickly shattered when I realized I was homeless. The housing that I thought was secure wasn't available to me. I didn't know what to do. The easy thing to do would have been to go back home with my head down in defeat.

That wasn't an option I would allow myself. I had to be resourceful and curious. I asked questions and started figuring it out. Are there spaces available on campus? The gravity of my situation didn't fully hit me because of my naivete. My vision of the life I wanted was so strong. I had no fear of the unknown because I had strong convictions. I told myself you got two options: Go to a shelter or go to the YWCA that folks are talking about. The YWCA sounded like the best option.

The Culture Shift...

My innocence was smashed. The veil was lifted, my perspective forever changed. The vision I had of NYC was getting murky, but the lessons were priceless. *I learned to trust the process.*

The Breaking Point...

The monitors are going crazy; the noise is unbearable. Doctors and nurses are rushing in. They are yelling, "Code blue!" They push me into the hallway. The moment I was waiting for to finally hold my baby turned out to be my breaking point. I stood there all alone, looking in. I started to cry uncontrollably as I watched the team try to resuscitate my little, tiny girl. You know the kind of cry I mean. That nasty, ugly cry with the snot running down your face. Yes, that one. My thoughts are going wild. All the fears, uncertainty, and anxiety that I was pushing down started rising to the surface and spilling over uncontrollably. I am in the deepest, darkest despair.

Until that point, I had kept up the facade of the ultimate badass. That's when one of the nurses came over and touched my hand. She said, "I've never seen you this way."

"I know this is tough; I know this can be insufferable… This is what we do; everyone in that room has one goal - to take care of your baby. We can't tell you everything will be OK because we don't know, there is no certainty. Things can change very quickly. What I can tell you is that you are not alone. Everyone in this NICU is going through a shared experience.

Take a look down the hall. What do you see? Do you see those white roses on the doors?" I moved my gaze from the room for a second and looked down the hall. I saw the white roses. She said, "Do you know what they mean?" I tried to talk through my tears. She said, "We put up a white rose when a baby is no longer with us. It is a gesture of remembrance."

"If you looked in those rooms, you would see babies that are no longer with us. We give time to the families to be with their babies. Time to say their final goodbye. Many of these families come from rural areas that don't have access to great health care. Some of those babies look perfect, but they have their own struggles. Some are born with no working kidneys or born without the front part of their brain."

Leadership Principle I | Change Your Lens

She said, "Your baby is a micro-preemie, and she has a long road ahead, but she has all her parts working." She mentioned the importance of perspective.

Here's the Leadership Principle I learned… "Change Your Lens" I was so focused on my perspective, on my pain, on my loss, and had blinders to others around me that were also on that shared journey. I had walked by those rooms and seen the roses on the doors, but I wasn't aware of what they meant, what others so close were experiencing.

Changing my lens required me to get out of my head and become *present*. It wasn't easy, but it was powerfully helpful at the time. I was able to experience a heightened level of empathy and gratitude. I started to be **Present and Intentional** with my actions, giving, serving, helping others as they navigated their storms. The more I focused on others, the more *abundance and gratitude* I felt. I felt like I was no longer on this journey alone. My perspective was forever shifted.

I also learned that helping others and serving is how we can *start to heal*.

The Unexpected Win

As I changed my lens and became present, I was able to also change my lens on fear. Here's the secret... **Being Present**. Is one of the keys to eliminating and reducing fear. Merriam-Webster defines fear as "an unpleasant emotion caused by *anticipation* or awareness of danger." The word I want you to notice here is **"Anticipation."**

Too many of us are crippled with fear, and it impacts our lives. I know because I have felt it too. It feels like your chest is being crushed, and sometimes it is hard to catch your breath. As I reflect on it, it truly is tied to the anticipation of the future, the story we create, or what others have created for us. That simple practice of being present and open to other perspectives changes your relationship with fear. You get to redefine negative anticipation to curiosity and limitless possibilities.

Reflection Point:

- What perspectives can you be open to?
- What stories are you holding on to?
- What fears are you anticipating?
- What negative emotions are you creating, and how can you reframe them?
- What is the true story?

These powerful questions allowed me to "change my lens on fear."

Leadership Principle II | Pull the Plug

The noise was finally subsiding, and I was starting to calm myself. The nurse asked me, "What are you doing to take care of yourself? You have a critical role to play; I know it is sometimes hard to see it now but to play that role, you have to take care of yourself." I shrugged my shoulders; the truth was I was stuck in my head. I felt immobilized with all the emotions; I was trapped in a loop of guilt, blame, and complaining. I told the nurse what I was struggling with. I told her, "I have so many thoughts going through my head I can't even sleep."

She looked at me with understanding in her eyes and said, "Here's what I want you to do. Get a notebook and start journaling your thoughts. Get everything out of your head. Nothing is off-limits. There are *lots of things you can't control*, but there are *lots you can*. You need to take time to *sort it out*." This simple statement led to the discovery of the next leadership principle. "Pull The Cord"

I took her sage advice and started journaling my thoughts and thinking of what I could control and what I couldn't control. I did this daily… every time I had a fear or negative thought, I would write it down and ask myself questions. "What stories am I telling myself?" "What excuses am I giving?" "What am I anticipating?" "What's true?" "What do I control?" "What can I do?"

This simple practice allowed me to "Pull The Plug"… I started becoming aware of my thoughts and reframing them from negative to empowering.

For example… **"I Have To"** was replaced with **"I Get To"**… Here's what I know… We all have choices; we don't have to do anything. That easy reframe allowed me to shift to a mindset of abundance. **"Why Me"** was replaced with **"Yes Me."** *I am strong and powerful. My past struggle has prepared me for this season.* This was an affirmation I said to myself on repeat. The more I said it, the more ingrained it became. I wrote my affirmations everywhere.

I "Pulled the Plug" on the negative emotions and limiting stories that were no longer serving me, and I gave myself permission to release them. I started visualizing the outcome I was creating. I got clear on my goals, my vision, and the new identity that I needed in this season.

If you're struggling with limiting beliefs... Know this. They aren't true (they just feel true because our brains love to find evidence to show us that it is). They are just thoughts. They can be replaced. They must be replaced.

Here Are a Few Reframes to Get You Going...

I'm not enough → I am enough

I can't → I am capable

It's too hard → It is easy if I break it down

This **mindset shift** will change your life...

I took responsibility for what I could control through my consistent journaling and reflection points. I could control my choices, feelings, thoughts, and how I prioritize my time. I took ownership of my new identity and knew my value. I realized that I couldn't help my daughter if I didn't take care of myself. If I wasn't strong physically and mentally, I couldn't be there for her, or my two kids in NY, my husband, or other Moms I grew to love.

I also "Pulled The Plug" and asked for help. In my check-in call with my leader, I asked to return to my role full-time and on my terms. I knew the journey was going to be a long one. I started to see things clearly and have honest conversations with myself. The reality was I had to relocate to Dallas, and there was nothing I could do about it. It was outside of my control. My daughter's journey was outside of my control.

I decided to go back to work because I wanted to do something I knew I was good at until my baby was ready to come home. I took on a massive initiative that provided me the flexibility to work remotely. I used my voice and asked what I wanted which was to get my entire maternity leave when she was strong enough to leave the NICU. I would have just pushed through and not asked for what I wanted in the past.

Here's the deal... You are stronger than you think. You have the power within you. Give yourself permission to "Pull The Cord" and take 100% responsibility for what you can control and release what you can't. Use your voice and ask for what you need. Ask for help. Over-communicate, prioritize yourself, and express your boundaries clearly.

I asked for help but shared my boundaries. I felt an unbelievable pressure to always say yes and not prioritize myself. Yes, was my default setting. I felt like I always needed to prove myself. Pulling the cord allowed me to release the limiting beliefs and fully embrace my power. Take the time to do the work. I have created free resources to help you at: LimitlessWomen.Gifts/Own-Your-Struggle

As a business owner, I've now realized that getting help is how I could have exponential growth and freedom. You can have a limitless life and have it all, but you can't do it all. *Asking for help demonstrates your leadership*.

Reflection Point:

- What do you need to "Pull the Cord" on?
- What's an empowering affirmation you can use to shift your thought process?
- Is there an identity or life blueprint that is no longer in alignment and negatively impacts you from your next level?
- Where are you giving away your power by holding on to excuses and stories?

I know asking yourself these questions isn't easy, but it's required to break through to your limitless future.

Leadership Principles III | Ride the Wave

The numbers were trending down; emotions were high. I thought, "When will this end? It's just one obstacle after another. She was born at 1.5 pounds, and now she is 1.3 pounds; it just doesn't make sense." I asked the doctor questions on her weight and the trends I noticed on the board. She walked over to the board and looked at me, and said, "Yes, her weight is trending down, and now we get to be curious and figure it out and take the required actions. That's why we have boards in every room. It's a way for the family and us to be on the same page. It's a cue on what's working and what's not working. It allows us to investigate what's triggering the event so we can take decisive action." I started taking pictures of the board, seeing the trends and actions the team was taking.

I was mesmerized by the simplicity of this system. The accountability that was created on the team to the families. The visual tracking of the critical metrics allowed everyone on the team to be focused on the ultimate goal. I started watching how seamlessly each staff member made their way to the board at the start of their shift, made updates, and cross-checked the system. They celebrated the wins and used the lows to identify what needed to shift. Interestingly, *it's usually the tiny shifts that get the maximum results.*

I learned firsthand the importance of monitoring, tracking, celebrating, learning, pivoting, and the power of enjoying the process. This consistent tracking process of critical and high-impact areas allowed the NICU team to care for some of the most critical infants. This system allowed them to "Ride The Wave" and deal with all the uncertainty that came with confidence and grace. I was inspired to get my own board for my apartment and started tracking my critical metrics — the needle movers for my own job and life. I started creating systems to streamline my process; I celebrated the small wins and learned from the lows. I learned to take decisive action with confidence, knowing that if something isn't working, I get to be curious and figure it out.

Here's a quick example of what I tracked on my personal board...

My **MEDS** (I learned this from one of my coaches)

- Meditation or Tapping

- Exercise: I walked every day — it was my time to get centered and set my intentions for the day. I still do this consistently for a min of 30 mins every day. This is one of my non-negotiables.

- **D**iet: I don't follow a diet plan; I practice conscious eating.

- **S**leep: This is a critical one that was so hard for me until I leveraged my journaling to help me relax and unwind from the day. Once that routine was firmly in place, I was able to enjoy the benefits of a good night's sleep finally.

I have created free resources to help you do this, too, at: LimitlessWomen.Gifts/Own-Your-Struggle

Reflection Point:

- Are you tracking your vital metrics in your life and business/career? (Goals, vision, and results you want to achieve.)

- Are you connecting with your emotions, embracing them, and releasing them? (Emotions are meant to be felt, then expressed.)

- Where do you need to "Ride the Wave?"

- Are there systems and processes you can implement to help you "Ride The Wave?"

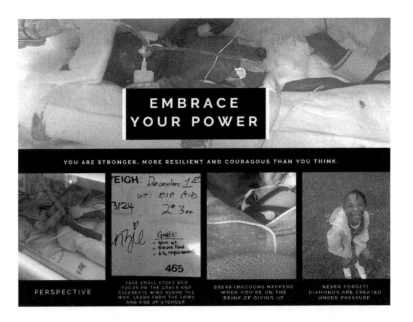

Leadership Principle IV | Connect The Dots

"You can't connect the dots looking forward; you can only connect them looking backward. So you have to trust that the dots will somehow connect in your future."

—Steve Jobs

I love this quote; it is *So True*. Every struggle that I experienced in the past prepared me for this season. That year I was awarded "The Elite Award" for the results I produced during one of the most challenging times in my life.

Over the next five years, I did a deep dive into figuring out how to win at both business and life.

I knew there had to be a way to kick ass at work and still have all the time I wanted to spend with my loved ones and still take care of myself. I took courses, I went to workshops, I got a coach, I hired, and I learned from lots of experts; I can tell you — not everything worked, but I figured out what did work for me. I learned from the best of the best and became a certified high-performance success coach.

I was able to figure out how to not just survive but THRIVE and 10X my results in business and life. Now instead of just thinking, "I'm a badass," — I actually am that badass! I now work fewer hours, get bigger results than ever, and I spend quality time with people I love most.

As a certified high-performance success coach and business and life strategist, I have the tools, resources, and business acumen to help multiply your results without burnout, stress, or overwhelm. I am committed to helping you unleash your power, develop an unshakable mindset, manifest your vision through clarity of purpose, and create momentum through simple systems, processes, and habits that lead to sustainable results.

And the results from my clients have been exceptional.

As a Mother and Businessperson...

- I believe you can win at work.

- I believe you can win at business.

- I believe you can win in life and have it all because you are limitless.

I don't want you to live an unfulfilled life where you're overworked and miss out on quality time with your loved ones.

Because as someone who had a near-death experience, I would be the first to tell you that spending more time at the office was not something I wanted to do.

Take the first step by reaching out to me at FeleciaEtienne.com, and let's get started with your journey!

Felecia Etienne

Felecia Etienne, MBA, CHPC, is a High-Performance Success Coach and the Founder and CEO of Level Up and Thrive Coaching and Consulting, who helps overwhelmed and stressed out leaders maximize their time, energy, and productivity so that they can be present and intentional with the vital areas of their life.

With two decades of experience working with Fortune 500 Global Financial Services companies, she has coached over 1500 high-performing leaders, executives, and business owners. However, she's not stopping there! With a goal of empowering 500,000, Felecia is on a mission to help business owners, leaders, and ambitious professionals reclaim their power while creating a profitable legacy. Her proven strategies, tools, and business acumen can help anyone level up their life or business on their own terms.

Her coaching journey started when she was an overstressed professional who had a near-death experience while giving birth to her third child. As a result, she dove headfirst into a discovery process to learn how to win at both business and life without having to choose one over the other.

As a certified high-performance success coach and business and life strategist, she now helps others discover the same through her proven three-step process. If they're in the early stage of their business or career, or they're already established, her clients see their bottom-line results multiply, find an increase in overall productivity, and discover resilience without burnout, stress, or being overwhelmed with her methods.

For more information on Felecia's current programs and free resources to help you Level Up and Thrive in your life and business/career so you can be more present and intentional with the vital aspects of your life, visit FeleciaEtienne.com.

Felecia Etienne's Credentials:

- Certified High-Performance Coach trained by Brendon Burchard
- Certified Success Principal Trainer and Coach trained by Jack Canfield, also a Mastermind Lead for Jack.
- Performance Coach trained by Jerrick Robbins
- Mastermind Professional trained by Tony Robbins and Dean Graziosi

Felecia Etienne
Level Up and Thrive Coaching and Consulting
455 Tarrytown Road, Suite #1169
White Plains, NY 10607
Felecia@FeleciaEtienne.com
FeleciaEtienne.com

The Limitless Women Resilience Workbook

The Limitless Women Resilience Workbook is designed to help ambitious women just like you become more resilient. This workbook is packed with reflection exercises and activities that will help you overcome your obstacles, reach your goals, and become the best version of yourself.

Start living the life you deserve with this workbook. It's time to OWN YOUR STRUGGLE!

https://LimitlessWomen.Gifts/Own-Your-Struggle

Joy Cooper

Flying, Falling, and Fighting: A Journey of Recovery

"A witness located near the intersection of the Seward and Sterling Highways stated that he was outside shortly after 4 pm when he heard an airplane flyover. He said it sounded like the airplane was flying west to east and as if it was 'maneuvering under power.' He stated that this lasted for about 15 seconds before all sound ceased. An Air National Guard Pavehawk crew discovered the accident site, and the sole survivor was subsequently evacuated."

—National Transportation Safety Board Preliminary Report

Every alarm and warning imaginable rang in my ears as our plane tossed through the air. The co-pilot door flew open at the sudden jerk. The air that was already tense and filled with smoke blurred over, as the pilot struggled to gain control. The plane leveled for a few seconds before it jerked straight up and fell into what lay below.

I woke up thinking we were back at Allen and Kelly's house in Anchorage. My ears were ringing, and my head was spinning. The air smelled strangely fresh, like tilled soil and trees. All I could see was shrubs, dirt, and glass shards. For a moment, I was convinced I was sitting on the floor, watching an old war movie. The dirt, trees, broken glass, and twisted metal somehow reminded me of the jungles of Vietnam in *We Were Soldiers*. The whirling of the plane's instruments caught my attention as they spun to a stop. My eyes looked around as my head stayed completely still, as if I was frozen in place.

A high-pitched beep pulled me out of my dazed imagination. I realized that we were not back at the house. Our floatplane had fallen from the sky and crashed into the side of a mountain. For now, I was still alive. I blinked, trying to focus. My immediate fear was that the plane would burst into flames. The smell of earth and clean air helped to ease that fear just a little bit. I knew I shouldn't move, in case my neck or something drastic was broken, but I had to know what happened and try to get help.

I turned my head gingerly and began to take in everything. My shoulder harness had unclipped and swayed eerily with every movement I made. I turned to see that the pilot, Allen, was alive but severely injured and unconscious. I strained to see Kelly and Claire in the back. I yelled their names in the deafening silence, yet they didn't stir or respond. I saw Claire's head of beautiful, brown curls slumped against the back of Allen's seat, and I knew she was gone. I couldn't see Kelly, who was sitting right behind me, but assumed she was also gone. Considering the amount of pain they could have experienced, the rational part of me was relieved they didn't even know what happened.

Turning to face the shattered windshield in front of me, I lifted my arm to push my door open and get help from below. My upper arm rose to my command, but my forearm swung free like a pendulum. Well, I thought, *There's my first injury*. The skin was completely split and every bone in my elbow was shattered. Large drops of blood fell on my brand-new pants, as I begged my arm to help me escape.

I decided to take advantage of my few minutes of pain-free shock to get out and slide down the mountain to find help. The pool of blood gathering on my shirt told me it was now or never. Since my elbow was as useful as a spaghetti noodle, I fixated on my fingers and willed them climb up the dashboard of buttons and instruments. My forearm advanced as instructed, until I had pulled my upper arm around the windshield's frame. I let out a guttural cry and pulled with all my might as a sharp pain tore through my chest and back. When I let go, I sank back the short distance I gained. Four times I walked my fingers up, over, around, and pulled, breathing through the pain, hoping I would break free. I leaned against the seat, exhausted, hopeless. There was no way to get out of the plane.

We had crashed somewhere in the Alaskan wilderness. It would take hours for even the most experienced rescue team to arrive. I found a popped-out instrument, slumped over, using it as a pillow, and took a nap. Deep down, I knew I'd need every ounce of energy and determination to survive what came next

Before the Fall

Claire and I had flown out to Alaska four days before to visit her Uncle Allen and Aunt Kelly. They were excited to show us Alaska in the summer, and we had been looking forward to flying, hiking, and taking in the peaceful, bold wilderness. I was looking forward to flying Allen's floatplane, if he'd let me. We spent three days at their lake property boating, hiking, seal watching, and four-wheeling.

The morning before we left to fly back to Anchorage, Claire, Allen, and I had finished a hike to the waterfall on the other side of the lake, absorbing the last beautiful day of peace, quiet, and no cell signal. Kelly had spent the morning bird watching by the cabins, and Allen made one last call on the satellite phone to verify the weather along our route. Satisfied, we loaded the floatplane and climbed in.

I slid into the co-pilot seat, and Kelly tapped me on the shoulder, "Put your shoulder harness on." I always forgot those. The day couldn't have been more perfect. We took off over the bay, into a cloudless sky. I was able to fly after takeoff until Allen exclaimed, "Hey, look! Orcas!" He took the controls and flew us low over the water. We circled over the small pod of whales a few times. Two adults and a little calf swam close to the surface. After a few turns, we leveled out and climbed back toward the mainland.

As we flew inland, a thin layer of smoke had settled over the end of Kenai Lake. A large wildfire to the west of the area had been burning for weeks and frequently covered the area with a light haze. When we left Anchorage three days before, it was a little smoky, so we weren't worried about it becoming any worse. However, the further inland we flew, the thicker the smoke became; until, in what felt like seconds, we couldn't see anything outside the plane. We had just entered a mountain pass and had no way of turning around without risking smashing into the trees.

Allen kicked into action, cross-checking the instruments, and directing the rest of us to look out the windows for trees and terrain.

Persistent alarms began going off, "Terrain, Terrain, Pull up, Pull up."

Allen wasn't fazed by the alerts. He knew the mountains were close to us and was intentionally flying near them to be able to turn around. I had no idea where we were in relation to anything. I knew about the dangers of flying into poor visibility conditions but never experienced them. Statistically, we had 90 seconds to break free.

Allen kept a hawk-eye gaze on his iPad ADS-B map and the rest of his instruments as he frantically tried to turn us around, out of the mountain pass. Just before we broke free of the smoke, to everyone's horror, the plane violently pitched up and to the left. My door flew open. I instinctively reached out to close the door as the plane continued to be tossed like a salad. The plane then pitched up again, followed by a sinking feeling in the pit of my stomach. The floating, weightless feeling followed by a high-pitched, monotone stall warning confirmed the worst. I said a silent prayer, hoping beyond hope that we would make it through. I heard the reassuring voice of God telling me, "You're going to be okay," and I relaxed.

Rescue!

The sound of a helicopter flying low overhead woke me up. My head was resting on the GPS that had popped out from the dashboard. *Thank you, Lord! They finally located the plane and can get us out of here!* The sound passed over and away, and I wanted to shout, *Wait, no! Over here! You're so close!* Instead, I leaned myself against the seat and prayed that they would come back. Allen stirred at my movement, but his breathing was slow and shallow. The Pavehawk circled two more times before steadily hovering a little bit away. I waited until I heard footsteps in the brush and pleaded, "Help! There are still people alive!"

I don't know about you, but I'm always happy to see a man in uniform. When Bryan walked around the front of the plane, I don't think I've ever been more relieved. I heard someone else behind me, opening the back door. I propped myself up with my newly discovered broken left wrist and shattered but operable right arm. Blood covered almost everything. I looked at Bryan and tried to give the most thorough, quick briefing of what I knew.

"My name is Joy. The two in the back are dead. He is still alive but barely holding on. I think he broke his neck and has a bad gash in his head. My right arm is broken, and my legs are trapped."

Bryan nodded, "Okay, don't worry. We're here with the National Guard, and we're going to get you out."

That's pretty cliché, I thought, but I didn't care one bit! Allen was holding on like a true captain, giving it all he had. Unfortunately, he passed away shortly after the guys arrived.

The pararescueman behind me, Jimmie, spoke calmly. "She's right. They are both gone back here. The only way we can get her out is to cut off the top, get to the bolts on her seat, and pull her out that way."

I heard a small saw start up and knew there would be sparks from cutting the metal. My brother was a firefighter and did vehicle evacuation demonstrations for safety events, so I knew the drill.

"Sorry, I don't have anything to cover you with. There's going to be some sparks, but it won't be for long." Jimmie warned.

"That's okay," I replied as I turned my head away. "I know what you have to do. Don't worry about me." I muttered to myself, *I don't care how many metal burns or scratches I get. Just get me OUT OF THIS PLANE!*

I turned my head away and closed my eyes. I thought I was just resting, but the guys immediately realized that I was in a much worse condition. I had lost a lot of blood and only had a small window of time left. They knew it had already been over three hours since the plane crashed, and the closest hospital was a 30-minute flight away. As they put it later, I was "circling the drain" with only their expertise and speed to keep me from being sucked under.

Fighting to Stay Alive

Bright lights shone overhead, as shadows danced over me. Distant voices hit my ears as the emergency techs were quickly discovering I wasn't much more than a pile of broken bones.

"Here," someone with authority called out. "Head laceration. I need some staples."

Three clicks to the head later, I was unconscious again. When I woke, I struggled to breathe, gagging on something stuck in my throat. A nurse rushed over as I tried to pull the tube out. She tied my arm down, as I inwardly protested, *haven't I already been through enough?* An increase of medication quickly put me back to sleep.

I hadn't even begun to grasp how narrowly I escaped death or how badly broken my body was. I hadn't only broken my wrist and elbow. No, I had shattered every extremity. A broken rib punctured my lung, and my L1 vertebra was completely crushed. I was paralyzed from the waist down from four spinal cord tears. My ankles were so badly crushed and torn that the blood loss and muscle damage almost caused me to lose my left foot. Through fervent prayer, God restored the muscle, and I kept both feet.

The next five days were filled with multiple surgeries, delirium, and agonizing pain. I've been told I was keeping up with everything, carrying on conversations, and whisper-yelling at people to not touch my bed. I remember very little.

A week after the accident, the thick veil over my mind cleared. The pain wasn't completely blinding anymore. I could remember more than the past five minutes. My condition changed from critical to stable, and I moved up to acute neurosurgical care.

I still couldn't move. I had external metal rods screwed into what bones I didn't break to keep me together, making movement even more impossible. My mom and sister had flown up to Alaska as soon as they heard about the accident and were there with me around the clock.

The surgeon allowed me a week and a half free of surgeries before removing the Frankenstein-esque external fixators and screwing me back together. Three surgeries later, my right arm and ankle were in a cast, and my left ankle was in a large, metal apparatus meant to get bone fragments to grow back together. Even with my right side free, I found I couldn't even sit up by myself. My once strong core muscles were non-existent. I couldn't feel my hips or legs to provide any balance. I joked with the nurses that I would be moving my toes by the end of the day, but it was more than a joke. I knew someday it would happen no matter what anyone said.

Journey to Recovery

Before the accident, being active was a way of life for me. I was independent and motivated to climb the corporate ladder as an airline operations manager. Aviation was in my blood. I earned my private pilot's license before I graduated from college and had just started my master's degree in aerospace operations.

Outside of work, dancing was my favorite way to de-stress. I took ballroom dance classes for two years and participated in showcases and freestyles. A magical waltz would sweep away all my stress. My dance group became my community. They were my fun, peaceful outlet of emotion. Everything was going as planned. I was on track to reach my social and corporate goal of becoming a director at a major airline, but God had other plans.

As I laid in that hospital bed, all I could think about was dancing on Tuesday nights. I obsessed over it. I even suggested to my surgeon that he amputate the troublesome ankle and give me a prosthetic, because if he fixed my ankle and it couldn't move, I wouldn't be able to dance again. As expected, he was a little concerned about my sanity! I always believed I would dance again, that I would get back to some form of normal, and this would just be another story to tell. Thankfully, my surgeons in Alaska, my family, and support group also believed I would walk and dance again and posted their encouragement with the hashtags #tinydancer and #shewilldanceagain. Six weeks after the accident, I was able to move my right toe.

The mind is a powerful thing. I never thought that I could control an arm that was completely shattered and dangling or that hope and prayer could heal four spinal cord tears and refute the diagnosis of many professionals. I am here to tell you that they can! I had to push harder and more creatively than my therapists could make me. I had to dig deep into what I knew was true to prove to myself and others that I would overcome any limitation.

When I was finally discharged from the hospital, four months later, it still wasn't a pretty picture. My mom's main goal was to fatten me up with good home cooking. I weighed ninety pounds and had to use a wheelchair. Nevertheless, I could hop. I could hobble on my one good foot while the rest of me continued to heal.

Seven months after the accident, I flew back home to Virginia. Life could finally get back to "normal." I was so excited to be able to see my coworkers and show off how far I'd come. March 2020, I was cleared to return to work, but then COVID happened. When I finally returned to work, I couldn't wipe the smile off my face! My coworkers had been my cheering squad during recovery and some had taken the accident almost as hard as my family. It was a moment we had all been looking forward to.

Dancing was harder to accomplish. My left ankle doesn't move, and my right ankle likes to flop around like a fish. That hasn't killed my passion though. Two and a half years later, I went out on a Tuesday night and danced again.

Accepting My Condition

I never thought I'd have to face being the only survivor of a plane crash or wonder whether I'd ever walk again. The last few moments of that fateful flight, I remember feeling a peace that everything would be okay. During my recovery, I often asked myself, *What part of any of this is okay?!* Then I realized I am okay. No, I won't be able to backpack mountains any time soon or gracefully waltz a dance floor, but I am alive and can encourage and inspire others to also overcome their "impossibles."

The title of this book is *Overcoming Mediocrity — Limitless Women.* My limits have obviously changed, but my perspective on life has grown. My trauma doesn't define me. My response determines my outcome. I've learned a few tips that I'd love to share.

1. Remember What You Love.

I love dancing, music, and adventure. I listen to music practically every free moment. My poor car has heard some terrible karaoke! Somehow during recovery, I forgot how much I loved and needed music. On a particularly bad day, my brother sent me a song. Immediately, I felt a cloud lift away. How could I have forgotten my routine before the crash?! I had fallen into a routine of medication, therapy, and adjusting. After I remembered my love of music, I also began watching old dance videos and purposefully connecting with friends. Those actions pulled me out of my routine, reminded me of what I was capable of, and connected me with the world outside the hospital.

2. Make Flexible Goals.

I am a very Type A person, so I don't say this lightly. While goals may be a lead brick to others, goals are a fun challenge for me. Two weeks after my crash, I told my boss I'd be back to work in two months. He got a good chuckle from that. When September rolled around, I was still in the hospital with at least two surgeries to go and could barely able to move my right leg. Before the accident, not being able to meet my goal would have broken my spirit. Thankfully, I learned early in the recovery process to make flexible goals. I had to change my mindset to use goal-setting as a way to encourage myself with something to work toward. Some days, my goal was to wake up and wash my face. Other days, it was to defy everyone's expectations and stand on my own. When my deadline approached, I didn't look at my failures. I looked at how far I'd come and set another goal.

3. Don't Forget Those Who Helped You Along the Way.

Just a few months ago, I went back to Alaska. I returned to the same mountains that changed my life forever and to the same people who poured into my family and me. God had told me I would be okay, and I never doubted that for one second. Others did not have that reassurance and were doubtful of my recovery. I wanted to show them that all their prayers and hard work paid off: I can walk and dance! I toured the National Guard base that dispatched Bryan, Jimmie, and the others to our crash site. The guys often visited while I was in critical care and were a constant source of encouragement and smoked salmon. I was able to walk around their base and see the behind-the-scenes of their missions. I could share with them my appreciation, and they could see the result of their hard work. Being able to walk and talk with those who had such a great impact on my life reminded me of what I had overcome and how truly limitless this life can be.

*The names of those involved in the crash were changed to protect their privacy.

Joy Cooper

Adventure, focus, and dedication changed the course of Joy's life when she was the sole survivor of a fatal plane crash. Joy Cooper was born and raised in Paris, TX and currently lives in Sterling, VA. She works for United Airlines as an airport operations manager and has been involved in aviation since she was young. She firmly believes that her Christian faith and life experiences prepared her for this very moment.

Just this year, Joy graduated with a M.S. in Aeronautics from Embry Riddle University, specializing in aerospace operations and space systems. She also holds a B.S. in air traffic management from LeTourneau University, has her private pilot license, and holds an aircraft dispatch certificate. If you couldn't tell, she loves aviation and travel!

As a result of working in airline operations for eight years, Joy has intimate knowledge of the safety protocols, training, and different facets of maintaining safe operations. Only a week after her life-changing crash, a well-meaning counselor mentioned that she may be afraid to fly again, to which she replied, "That is the stupidest thing I have ever heard." She believes that when you love something, you don't let anything get in your way.

Joy's story of recovery and growth from a serious tragedy is one of determination and realization of those things that are truly important. While she has been recovering, Joy has given safety talks to aviation classes regarding her crash and hopes to continue to provide perspective and warning to fellow aviators. Her goal is to use her experiences to inspire others and help them define what limitless means in their life. She is currently working on a full book of her story.

Joy Cooper
Sterling, VA
Info.JoyCooper@gmail.com
JoyCooper.org

The Moose Pass Crash Challenge

Answer these ten questions to see if you would survive the Moose Pass Crash. After completing the quiz, you will have the option to download the NTSB investigation report for the crash. As the sole survivor and pilot-rated passenger of that flight, my goal is to share the events surrounding that crash with aviation community members to prevent future errors.

https://JoyCooper.org/moose-pass-challenge

Jackie Geisler

Discovering Unconditional Self Love

Do you know that feeling when you first tell someone you're in love with them? It's a rush of nervousness and excitement. Maybe you've been thinking about it for weeks, or maybe it just came out unexpectedly. When you say those words, you feel a weight lifted off your shoulders. You feel on top of the world.

Have you ever felt that feeling when saying "I love you" to yourself for the first time? I've felt that. In June 2021, I found deep and unconditional love for myself for the first time ever. Since then, this newfound self-love has flourished into something juicer than I could have ever imagined. The woman I am today is a force. *I am a powerhouse. I find happiness every day. I've reclaimed my power.* I now create my life as I choose.

It's important to know that my life wasn't always this way. I invested and poured into myself to get to this place. I'd do it over again a million times because it's raw and sexy. It's me versus me.

Most of the time, my cup is full and overflowing. My intention is to take the overflow from my cup and help you fill yours, so that yours can also overflow. I want you to feel the magic that I do. **My mission on this earth is straightforward: to help as many women as possible find the healthiest, happiest, and most self-loving versions of themselves, while expressing myself as authentically as I can and filling my cup first every step of the way.**

Let's get crystal clear on how I got to where I am. However, it's worth bringing to your attention that everyone's journey is different. Your pace might be different from mine (slower, similar, faster, etc.), and that's perfect. You might tackle things in a different order or spend more time in one area than in another. Your journey is your journey, and that's good enough.

Where It Started

Going into college, I was in the best athletic shape of my life. I was recruited to play soccer and lacrosse while in school. The fact that I was a two-sport college athlete, however, did not mean that I was healthy. Being away from my parents for the first time and truly on my own was freeing but came with its challenges. Throughout my college career, I gained 30 pounds and struggled as a yo-yo dieter. I'd gain and lose weight like a pendulum. I developed a terrible relationship with myself, my body, fitness, and food. Before I knew it, I was binge eating, binge drinking, binge eating while drunk, and falling into a handful of unhealthy patterns.

Not only was I physically unhealthy, but I was also mentally unhealthy. I was always falling short of my own high expectations and then feeling frustrated with myself. Whenever it was time to get dressed to go to class or go out to the bar, my inner mean girl was unleashed. I smashed myself down with my words and thoughts. I made sure to keep myself small, sought external validation, and truly never felt satisfied with who I was or where I was in life.

This state of being physically and mentally unhealthy continued after college for quite some time. However, I was eventually able to get my physical health under control. My relationship with my body, food, alcohol, movement, and self-care has completely transformed. I can't say I am perfect in my health, nor do I want to be. After taking one step after another and trusting my intuition, I found a passion for fitness and nutrition as a career.

Who I was as a human changed because of improving my health. I knew I had to help other women feel and experience similar changes. I did network marketing, trained at a big corporate gym while getting my certifications, and eventually started my own women's health coaching company.

I was intentionally showing up by working out, eating clean, reading, journaling, setting goals, reflecting, and investing in coaching programs. You might think that someone taking this action day after day would be a superhuman with success, confidence, direction, and high levels of productivity. That's what I thought, but I wasn't.

Every day I'd pour into myself and pour into my business. Somewhere along the line, I became addicted to my business. My business ran the show and came before just about anything. It came before downtime, sleep, friends, socializing, and calling my family. It was my everything, yet I was still very unsatisfied every single day. I constantly told myself I wasn't good enough and I wasn't producing enough. If anyone resonates with this, then you know how debilitating it can be to feel constantly not where you want to be. I always felt stuck and like I was moving slower than I wanted to be. I began to get anxious any time the computer wasn't open. It took me out of my life. There was no living, only stressing and overthinking.

What had happened? Why did I feel like I wasn't able to move forward without friction? How was I sometimes working 10 to14 hour days, neglecting everything else in my life, but still feeling like I wasn't where I wanted to be?

It boiled down to these four things: I never felt good enough. I constantly felt stuck. I was neglecting everything in my life. I felt high levels of anxiety and discomfort, when stepping away from work.

When things were at their worst, I was forcing myself to follow a strict schedule. I had everything in my life mapped out by the hour in my Google calendar. I remember there being a day where I had 90 minutes scheduled for a workout followed by 30 minutes for a post-workout meditation, steam, and shower. I remember rushing myself through my workout to be done faster, while working on my phone in between every set. When it was time for my meditation, I could only sit still for two minutes.

In hindsight, yes, something is better than nothing. Two minutes of meditation instead of zero was good enough, but it still didn't sit well with me.

I was okay taking away from my social life, not having a lot of downtime, or even working on holiday weekends. What I wasn't okay with, was realizing my work was coming before MYSELF.

That's where I drew the line. Who was I to be cutting my workouts short? Why did I feel the need to work, while walking to and from the gym or waiting in between sets? Who am I to be neglecting the centering habits I'd worked so hard to create? I was teaching people to be healthy, and I thought I was healthy because I was physically healthy. I also thought that because I read personal development books, hired coaches, and journaled my goals, I was some kind of mindset guru when really, I wasn't going deep at all.

I was stressed, negative, overwhelmed, and unhappy with myself and my life. My dream job was the reality I created, but that still wasn't enough. Change needed to happen in order to get present in my life again.

Pay Attention to Your Thoughts

In April 2021, I set out with the goal of clearing through whatever it was that was blocking me. I went to Florida to spend a month alone. Unaware that this was a major missing element, I started the journey of learning to love myself. While in Florida, I worked through an emotional process of looking at every single conscious self-judgment I could think of that I held about myself. I forced myself to confront these judgments. Things like:

- You can't be happy now because you are always searching for future happiness elsewhere.

- You're always stuck making slow progress because you've experienced slow and difficult growth since you were young.

- You are not smart enough to build the business you want because you struggle to learn and grasp concepts. You break down easily when you don't understand something.

- You have to work extra hard to get the things you want because you have ALWAYS been one step behind.

- You are not special enough to be who you want to be. You should be further along.

- You suck at managing your time because you don't follow through. You always fall short of high expectations. You don't get enough done to be where you want to be.

These were some of the thought patterns I had while going into my month of isolation. I got super crystal clear on all the ways in my conscious awareness that I was limiting myself. This included negative thoughts, negative words, self-judgments, self-shame, self-blame, negative cycles, and anything else. Each night, I'd look myself straight in the mirror. With each belief, I'd repeat again and again… "Yes, in the past, I have judged myself as *XYZ*, and now I forgive myself" or "I forgive myself for judging myself as *XYZ*." I'd repeat the statement until I felt a physical, mental, or emotional opening of self-forgiveness. The opening for forgiveness came in many different ways. Sometimes it was a release of pressure off my chest or head. Other times it meant I started crying and let myself sob until it stopped. With enough intentional and authentic repetition, I learned that I could create raw and deep forgiveness for myself.

My next step was to create clarity on where these beliefs came from and on how they were holding me back. It was time for the self re-creation phase. I recreated my relationship to all of these thoughts. I decided what they meant to me, and I decided on a more powerful, yet not overwhelming, new association. I spent significant amounts of time with this entire process: forgive and recreate.

This was just the beginning. I'd created peace with my past limiting beliefs, but I knew I also needed to tackle my current and real-time thoughts. I had to become aware of how I was negatively judging myself on a day-to-day basis, in order to not let those automatic negative loops continue running my life. Looking back now, it's crazy to think I had to ask my coach at the time, "How do you remember to pay attention to your thoughts?" We spoke every single Wednesday, and towards the beginning of our work, when it came time for the call, I couldn't remember how I had talked to myself or what negative (or even positive) things came up.

Over the next few weeks and months, I learned how to regularly pay attention to my thoughts. I can confidently say that when you can raise awareness of the thoughts you are having, whether they are positive or negative, it's game over. **You have taken your power back**. You can celebrate the good and recreate how you relate to the negative. It's hard work at first, but once you get rolling, you're a powerhouse. The positive becomes addicting. When you see it, you acknowledge it, celebrate it, and bring light to it by focusing on it. It becomes easier to duplicate.

I started to live my life by thinking more thoughts that served me. I took anything that I didn't like. I either got rid of it or changed how I related to it. I fell in love with things in my life that I had previously resisted.

When you can raise your awareness of your thoughts, it's game over. It requires time, but if you can take the time, you hold the power. I truly believe there is no right way or perfect way to do these things. However, I will say this for what it's worth: **Just get curious**. Be gentle with yourself always but get curious.

Spend Time Alone

After my month alone in Florida confronting my thoughts and beliefs, I started to take advantage of every opportunity I could that allowed me to be alone. Any time I'd get asked to dog sit or house sit, I'd say yes. I started extending my morning and night routines again and found a sense of consistency I hadn't felt in a while. It felt rejuvenating to step away from work as much as I was and cherish my alone time and downtime once again. Nightly stretching sessions, bubble baths, journaling in bed, and getaway weekends became my new normal.

When I tell you that I fell in love with being alone, I truly mean it. I fell in love with the space it created. The space allowed me to slow down, reflect, let my intuition speak and be heard, let creative ideas flow, unwind, and deeply care for myself. I ultimately created the space for me to intentionally process my life every day as it was happening. I was creating space for myself to be as I needed to be and flow as I needed to flow.

I had gone from a Jackie that was frantic, stuck, negative, and addicted to work to a Jackie that was at peace more often than not. I was deeply nourishing, respecting, and caring for myself every single day. In fact, that entire summer, people kept saying their normal advice to me of "make sure you are taking time off." I remember thinking to myself, what? Why are you telling me this? I've worked three-day weeks all summer.

At this point, I now feel the need to address something: **Time**. You might be thinking something along the lines of, "Well, Jackie, that's great you had the ability to get away for a month and focus on your thoughts and find all this time to be alone, but that's not doable for me with my life because of my XYZ." If you haven't been reminded lately, there is no 100% right way to do or not do something. Your journey is your journey, and that's good enough. The order and pace at which you tackle things in your life is irrelevant, as long as you show up for yourself and challenge yourself.

With this being said, your journey will 100% look different than mine. We've covered how once I started to pay attention to my thoughts, it was game over. It was the "death" of old Jackie and the emergence of my higher self. We've also covered the beautiful blessing of time spent alone in my journey. I truly believe that these two points are CRUCIAL to finding higher levels of self-worth, happiness, positivity, self-compassion, and understanding. If you are here for this journey as well, you absolutely need to be intentional about your thoughts and words, and create space for yourself.

Be okay being imperfect. Things will always come up. Life is life. You have to learn how to show up for yourself deeply, no matter what is going on. Make the time and fill your cup because when your cup is overflowing, you can give that overflow to others. When your cup is empty, people will drain your cup lower. Understand and be okay that not everything will be a perfectly aligned opportunity to show up for yourself. However, that doesn't mean you can ignore yourself. Let those words sink in. That does not mean you can ignore yourself. If it's important to you, you will create the time and space.

Allow More

We have arrived at the final pillar of my journey: allow more. I fully attribute my growth in this area to the book, *The Big Leap* by Gay Hendricks. In *The Big Leap*, Gay talks about how as humans, we have a tendency to limit ourselves, keep ourselves stuck, or self-sabotage ourselves. This happens in many areas of our lives. However, the biggest example I can give is when you lose the first 10 of 30 pounds you want to lose. You then self-sabotage yourself and gain the weight right back. We have a natural tendency to only allow a certain level of success, health, wealth, and happiness in our lives.

You must fully believe that you are deserving of having more in your life. Having more of what? That's up to you, but you have to believe you are deserving, because you are. Your goals and desires were placed with you for a reason. Allow yourself to expand. When you become aware of how you are limiting yourself through your thoughts, words, beliefs, and actions, it becomes easier to break those things down and move into higher levels of health, happiness, success, and abundance.

The last thing I will say here is to allow more, not just once but forever. I don't say this to stress you out and make you think that you always have to be moving forward at 100% capacity at all times. What I am saying is, allow yourself to move forward always and forever. There is no limit. Know that you will forever be growing, and understand that there is NO END GOAL. This will allow you to be at peace with where you are in the journey and the pace you are moving at. You can love yourself as you have been, as you are, and as you will be.

Let's look back to the very first question I asked: Do you know that feeling when you first tell someone you're in love with them?

I felt that with myself and for myself. I set out in April with the goal of getting unstuck. Still, I didn't realize all I needed was to learn to love and accept myself deeply and unconditionally and that from there, everything becomes easier, more peaceful, and more authentic.

There was one day in June 2021 where I felt fully aware of the love that I had for myself for the first time ever. I was sitting on the couch, of course, by myself. It was a Friday, and previously that day, I got stuck in traffic. I was running behind, and I had to have a hard conversation with someone. These are all things that would have previously made me anxious, overwhelmed, and frustrated. However, at the end of the day, I wasn't. I felt happy moving through my everyday life. I had an overwhelming rush of emotions and happiness while sitting there. I wept like a baby because I was truly happy just existing and being present in my life. I was able to enjoy the little things again and find joy. I am forever proud of myself for creating space to forgive myself, recreate myself, nourish myself, and accept myself as I am.

Life can be so damn juicy and magical. When I say I have found the highest levels of happiness and alignment, that's not an exaggeration. I am in the best mental, emotional, physical, and psychological health I have ever been in. I love myself and feel called to show up now more powerfully than ever before because I have seen how my entire life has changed since then. I am an entirely different woman. I no longer tolerate things in my life that do not serve me or take more energy from me than they give me. I stand up for myself and my wants and needs in stronger ways than ever before. I see my mistakes as lessons and choose to be gentle with myself. I trust myself and my intuition in ways I never knew were possible. I find it easier to protect my energy and set boundaries. I expand in confidence the more I listen to myself and prefer to gently push myself in the direction of discomfort and insecurity. My brain has automatically shifted too easily and effortlessly to find the positives in almost any situation. As I said, it's juicy and magical.

I want all of this for you. If you decide you will create this reality for yourself, it's already yours. Please know that you are worthy of your desires, you are capable, you are deserving, and you are enough. Being enough for others, starts with first being enough for yourself and unconditionally loving you for you.

Jackie Geisler

Coach Jackie is your one-stop-shop for all things health, happiness, and self-love. She founded Live Free Fitness in 2019, with the mission of helping women change more than just their bodies. As a Certified Personal Trainer and Nutrition Coach, Jackie has helped hundreds of women find confidence, control, deep health, and more vibrancy for life. Since starting the company, she has changed her own mental, physical, and emotional health in even deeper ways. As a result, the vision for the company has shifted to something that's far bigger than just physical health and body composition change. Jackie helps women recreate how they are living their lives, how they are showing up, and how they are relating to themselves.

Jackie Geisler

Live Free Fitness

603-897-9950

Jackie@TeamLiveFree.net

https://LiveFreeFitness.co

Instagram: @Jackie_Geisler_Fitness

www.Facebook.com/Jackie.Geisler.9

Tiktok: @Jackie_Geisler_Fitness

4 Step Guide to Self-Forgiveness

Are you constantly bringing yourself down, judging yourself negatively, or getting in your own way? That doesn't have to be your reality. When I first started my self-love journey, I had to take a step back and look at all the ways in which I was getting in my own way or holding myself back. I was constantly judging myself and felt so stuck. It seemed like nothing was really moving forward, and I was just running into the same wall over and over again. In this 4 Step Guide to Self-Forgiveness, I will share with you my exact process for creating deep levels of self-compassion that kick-started my entire journey. This process will get you crystal clear on all the ways you hold yourself back, help you forgive yourself for those things, and powerfully recreate the ways you view yourself.

https://JackieGeislerFitness.activehosted.com/f/39

Sara Goggin Young

The Power to Believe™

For years, I had worked so hard to create a life that I loved and believed in. Two separate times, I literally had it ripped out from underneath me. The first time, I used all the wrong tools to feel good. The second time, I used all the right tools.

This is my story.

My toes were pressed against the wall. I saw the maroon and gold polish peek above the surface of the water, as I listened for the official to call us into position. My Sparky sticker tattoo looked to be laughing and dancing on my ankle, as I gazed straight ahead, getting into position for the 200 backstroke.

It was my junior year, at Arizona State University (ASU), at the Pac 10 Conference meet. I had prepared. I had trained thousands of yards a day, starts, turns, strength, flexibility, and mindset. I was ready. This was the PAC 10, the most competitive conference there is.

"Swimmers, take your marks! BEEP!"

I sprung off the wall, executing a perfect backstroke start, as my underwater kick propelled me to the front of the heat. I pulled my first stroke, popping out of the water. My turnover was quick, each stroke pulling me ahead and racing. Swimmers at Stanford, U of A, UCLA, and others were challenging me from the other lanes. Man, did I love this feeling of power and competition. My heart was in my chest as I turned the first wall, my lungs wanting to gasp for air. However, all my training kept me kicking underwater, until I came up to the surface. As I pushed forward, my legs were on fire! My body felt as if it would give up. I dug and dug, each stroke pulling me towards the finish line. Finally, I dove back and touched the wall.

Immediately looking up at my time, I was thrilled. My training had proved to my coach and me that I was on track to make the NCAA Finals and Olympic Trials my senior year.

A little over a month later, I planned a spring break trip with my roommate and teammate. We were going to hang out, relax, drink, eat, and be regular college kids. The trip started out fabulous, and we had way too much fun the first night. We got up early for a jog, when the guys we were staying with suggested instead, "Let's go water skiing!"

I had skied my entire life, and I jumped at the chance to be the first in the water. The slalom ski was different from the ones I was used to, strapping it on *before* I entered the water. I felt a tinge of worry. However, soon enough, I was up and zipping across the wake. Comfortable and confident, I prepared to jump the wake. I felt myself flying forward, but my ski did not.

"I f*%#ing broke my knee" was the continual loop in my head. I could feel nothing. It was like I was outside myself and my future immediately flashed before my eyes. I broke my knee — what does that mean for swimming?

"Goggin, come on!! Get up!! Let's go!!" The boys yelled from the boat. The girls were laughing, tanned shoulders were thrown back, bikinis in place, as the early morning haze was burning off.

I was in a sitting position, hands sculling beside me, with the water hugging everything in place. My voice sounded like a robot, "I broke my knee," I said again. My friend heard the shock in my voice, as he cocked his head towards me, showing a hint of concern.

"Goggin, you OK?"

"I broke my f#%!ing knee." I looked at him stunned, my face drained of color. He saw the terror in my eyes and quickly eased the boat behind me, so that they could lift me out of the water.

Grabbing the shoulders of the life jacket and gently pulling me up, the water that was hugging my leg began to pull it down, resulting in the most horrific and intense pain I have ever felt. Hot searing pain shot up and down my entire leg. One of the girls ran to the front of the boat and threw up, from just the sight of it.

I had hyperextended and dislocated my left knee. I tore my ACL, PCL, MCL, and LCL. I took a divot out of my femur, fractured my tibia, shattered my patella, and ripped all my cartilage. With that type of injury, amputation was a real possibility.

I was a 20-year-old driven athlete with dreams of the NCAA and the Olympic Trials immediately dashed. I had no one to turn to. I was alone, scared, and feeling like a total and complete failure. Everything I worked so hard to build was now gone.

I did the only thing I knew how to do to stop the pain. I pushed away my athlete friends, and I chose to self-medicate with alcohol and cocaine. My thoughts changed, my words changed, my habits changed, my character changed, and my destiny changed. Soon, I barely recognized who I once was. The entire trajectory of my life had changed.

I spent ten long years using drugs and alcohol to silence the whisper within me, before I did the work and got clean in 2004 (celebrating 18 years of sobriety in 2022!). There was a whisper that told me I was better than this, stronger than this, and I had so much to live for. I became unreliable, disloyal, and self-serving because I was consumed with how life was unfair — how this was happening TO ME. It was easy to keep drinking, using, and talking about all the things I could have accomplished yet never did. During that time, I no longer took pride in my body or being fit. I was drowning in poisons, even overdosing at one point. I lost friendships, job opportunities, family time, and more. I hurt people. And most importantly, I lost the Power to Believe™ in myself.

Foundation Rocked Again

"Do you understand if I stay, I will relapse and likely die? I am suffocating here."

I said this as my eyes searched my girlfriend's eyes. Tears fell freely, as I gasped for breath.

As soon as I got sober, I got married and had two beautiful children. However, it was messy. My marriage quickly became toxic, and I felt that I was failing as a mom. It seemed that no matter what I tried to do to improve my relationship and create the nuclear family I always strived for, it just didn't work. With that, my marriage quickly spiraled. I blamed my husband and everyone else for everything that didn't seem to be working correctly in my/our life together because that was the easy thing to do at first. However, once I chose to do the work to change the trajectory of my life, I found myself improving and finding my own strength, the right way and unsure that what I always dreamed would be my happy ending was still my truth. My foundation was rocked again.

Picture me, in my late-30s, as I cried myself to sleep every night (I thought no one knew I did), with my younger child asleep next to me and tears pouring silently from my eyes one night. I felt two soft hands on either side of my face.

"Mama? When is it your turn to be happy?"

That question took me aback. I couldn't think about it that night or the next morning. However, as the days and weeks started to fly by, I found myself thinking more and more about those sweet words from my baby boy. One night, I found myself rocking back and forth alone in my room, saying the serenity prayer, and feeling the despair of living in a toxic marriage. I was drowning in hopelessness, until I heard a voice. It was not from my head or heart, but from my soul. "Your children will never be happy, unless you are happy."

"It's OK. It is OK to leave," was the whisper deep within my soul.

I finally said out loud, "It's OK to leave. I deserve to be happy." I took my first deep breath in years, feeling a weight lifted off my shoulders. Little did I know this type of breath is called "The Goddess Breath," which is one of the Power To Believe™ tools I would come to use daily.

Letting Go

> *There is no weakness in forgiveness."*
> *Resentments are like pissing in your pants.*
> *You are the only one that feels them.*
> **(Read that again)**

When your pain is intense, awful, and heart-wrenching, what do you do? What I found was, just like the children's book I used to read to the kids… *There is no way around it, no way over it, no way under it. You must go through it. You must allow yourself to feel all of it, own it, surrender to it, and accept it in order to move through it.*

That is what I did when I chose to leave my husband and the family unit we created.

Everything I worked so hard for in my marriage felt like a lie. Feeling the pain of betrayal, whether it's emotional, physical, mental, or verbal, is excruciating. I knew I never wanted to feel that pain; that deep, soul throbbing, mind-consuming pain *ever again!*

That's where you begin. Pray over and again. Dig deep. Feel it. Own it. Surrender to it. Accept it. Then, and only then, can you put it down. By surrendering to and accepting exactly where you are, the hot mess of your life allows you to move on.

The first year after leaving my husband, I worked on learning how to forgive. Forgiving him, and forgiving myself.

I thought about my parents' divorce, the hatred, the drama, and the vile emotions we were raised with for so many years. Their divorce tore my brothers and sister apart and impacted all of our relationships to this day. My parents did the best they could with what they knew. However, I now know better, and I wanted better for my children and their father. I had experience with what happens to a family, if you cannot find forgiveness. I knew that if I truly wanted to put my children first, I must find forgiveness. So, I prayed. I prayed for strength and the ability to forgive. I believed that if I kept trying and showing up, my Higher Power would help me forgive.

The tools I used to let go of my failed marriage and rebuild myself into the woman I have always wanted to be, are the same tools I now use to coach others. They make up my coaching Power to Believe™ toolbox. In order to let go, we use the tools to create space within, connecting with our soul, to become centered in the midst of challenge.

Steps to Let Go:

Breath (7 Deep Goddess Breaths): This allows the body to dissipate emotions. Let your breath soften you, allowing you to respond instead of reacting.

Pray: Ask your Higher Power for the path to surrender and let go.

Feel Your Feelings: Lay them all out: pain, unfairness, hurt, and betrayal and step into them… let the ugly cries come. I'm talking about messy, hot snot, and so many tears running down your face, that there aren't enough tissues in the house.

Pour Love Within: Hold yourself as you wail, nurture your inner soul, and know that you are in the process of healing.

Empower Your Mindset

> *Your thoughts become your words.*
> *Your words become your actions.*
> *Your actions become your habits.*
> *Your habits become your character.*
> *Your character creates your destiny.*

I sat in the driveway of the first house I rented with my two kids after leaving my husband of 13 years. I had just dropped them off at school, and the silence of the moment called to me.

It was a crisp day, the ground frozen, the redbud tree had little icicles hanging from the branches, and snow clinging to the wood. The hummingbird feeder was hanging askew, reminding me of a task left undone.

Have you ever felt very alone in the middle of a vibrant, busy neighborhood? I felt as if everyone around me had "gotten life." They had received a memo that contained the secret sauce. They seemed happy, joyous, and free. I felt a stab of jealousy. I never received the memo.

So, I sat there in my car. I took my seven deep Goddess breaths, and I prayed.

The answer came not from my head but from my soul — my Higher Power. "You are good. Your heart is kind. You can achieve whatever you want, if you believe you can. All you must do is work for it. Change your mindset. Whatever you want, go after it. Follow the people that have done it. Model them. Do the work."

Work? I thought to myself, "I knew how to work!"

At that moment, I made a commitment to myself. I chose to become the strongest version of myself. The last time I felt that strong was when I was swimming, supported by a team when I had a coach and a plan.

A coach is someone who inspires and motivates you, while helping you create a plan to achieve your goals. A team is a group of people who work together, supporting each other, while moving towards a common goal. I found both. I did the work.

Single mom with two littles in bed, I woke each morning at 4:30 am, kissed my sweet baby's goodbye, drove downtown, and trained. Every day, I saw the sunrise, felt strong and empowered, drove home to wake the kids, dressed, and fed them before getting them off to school. On weekends, I traveled to swim meets throughout the country. I started racing again.

I knew where I was and where I wanted to be. I simply wanted to collapse the obstacles. How can I get to where I want to be in the quickest time? Change my mindset.

I dove into self-development. Scientists have proven you can change your thoughts. If others can, why not me? I began studying and researching. I followed Tony Robbins, immersed myself in his training, and became certified in his programs. I hired life coaches and studied, researched, read, and implemented. I did the work. EVERY.SINGLE.DAY. If you want something badly enough, you do whatever it takes. I wanted more than anything else to love my life, my thoughts, and be as successful as my whisper within told me I could be.

Just like training physically every day, I also trained my mind every day. Every single time a negative thought came into my mind (they were non stop at first), I tapped my forehead with my pointer and middle fingers and immediately chose a thought of gratitude.

Repeat. Over and over again. I had a bruise on my forehead.

When I couldn't replace the negative thoughts, I laid down. I listened to a guided meditation. Pretty soon, those positive thoughts became my thoughts. I became stronger and more confident. I started to pour love into my broken heart.

The "I AM" statement is the most powerful statement that comes out of our mouths. Our children and their friends are listening, babies, kids, tweens, teens, other adults, and our very own souls hang on to every word we say about ourselves.

"I AM BEAUTIFUL.
I AM STRONG AND POWERFUL.
I AM SMART AND CAN LEARN ANYTHING.
I AM KIND, LOVING, GENEROUS, AND GIVING.
I AM VIBRANT AND HEALTHY.
I AM SEXY… (& we say that 2x, so we never forget it!) I AM SEXY!
I AM A BOSS, A CHAMPION, A WARRIOR, AND A BADASS!!"

Did I feel these greatest strengths at first? Hell no! It felt uncomfortable and narcissistic. Why? Because we are not conditioned to love ourselves and speak to our greatest strengths. We tell our family and friends these strengths without blinking. However, we do not tell ourselves.

Building your mindset is like building your bicep. Your brain is a muscle, and it requires conditioning every single day. In positive conditioning, you build belief.

Belief = The utter and total confidence in someone or something, even though you cannot see it.

Power To Believe™ = The utter and total confidence in yourself and your life, even though you cannot see the path in front of you. You can achieve this when you condition your brain with the Power to Believe™. Your outside circumstances won't change. Your perception does. Your internal strength, power, and intelligence are turned on! So, whatever you are presently going through, you can handle it with strength and grace.

Manifest Your Dreams

Visualize yourself as already accomplished in your goal — see yourself as that positive version of yourself. In order to get to my strongest self, I chose to do it in body, mind, and soul. First, it was physical — I started to train my body into superior strength. I trained with the fastest Masters team in Chicago. Next, I filled my body with premium nutrition. Finally, I started changing my negative internal dialogue, and I empowered my thoughts on a daily basis. Vision Board???

Now, it was time to race. I knew I still had to do something after all of these years between the college me and adult me. I never fulfilled my dreams of winning an elite competition. Yet, I believed I could win, and I hadn't yet achieved my goal.

Within 12 months, I had placed top three in all of my Masters events and set a national record in the 200-yard medley relay, achieving All-American status for the second time in my life. Yet there was more. I had qualified for an international swimming competition, the Pan Am Masters.

At the start of my training, I was a single mom, busting my ass to figure out how to become the strongest version of myself for my two babies and for me. I went back to the basics, coupled with the scientific knowledge of how manifestation works. I primed, visualized, and manifested. I also created a vision board with my goals, complete with images and words of what I wanted in my life. On that vision board, was a goal time of 27.6, a little off my lifetime personal best from college.

Every night, I visualized. I swam my race in my head. With absolute clarity, I pictured the start, entry, and each stroke, all the way to my finish. Then it was time. I was totally prepared, using all my tools.

They called us to the blocks. Standing there, I felt so powerful. I got into position, and the gun went off. My entry was perfect, my underwater kicking powerful, and my turnover quick as my body moved through the water. I kept following my coach's advice — hips up, chin back. The water was splashing everywhere. My entire body was burning with pain. My power grew, as I hit the flags with five strokes to go. I dug in and sped to a phenomenal finish. My body tingled as I heard, "Sara Goggin Young, first place! 27.6" — a new Pan Am Masters World Record for my age group, beating out the four age groups younger.

The time was real, and it was the exact time as the vision board I created 12 months ago.

Vision boards work because they reprogram the subconscious mind. We create our goals in our conscious mind, and then our subconscious mind goes to work. The subconscious mind does not know the difference between fantasy and reality. With vision boards, we create an imprint on our subconscious through visual images, repetition, and emotion attached to the images. Just by gazing at the vision board multiple times a day, you are reprogramming your brain to achieve exactly what is on the board.

There are three skills to master when it comes to mindset:

1. **Let Go:** Let go of negative emotions, by learning to surrender, accept and love yourself.

2. **Empower:** Rewire your mind, by filling it with gratitude and focusing on your greatest strengths.

3. **Manifest:** Create your destiny. Set your goals, visualize, and create a vision board. See yourself achieving all your goals.

If you are stuck, need a small or a drastic change… ***Quiet the noise, get out of your head, connect to your soul, and empower your life.*** Hire a coach to hold you accountable. That's what I did, and my life has been transformed. I'm thriving as a single mom and passionate about my life coaching business. I love creating workshops and tropical retreats for others to find their Power to Believe™.

Life is challenging, and some people have more challenges than others. That's OK. Life is not fair. Stop wasting time wishing it was or wishing hard times away. Life is beautiful and while challenges can be brutal, stepping through them with strength and grace allows you to truly embrace all the beautiful moments.

You are enough! You can change anything you want! It just takes work, time, and the Power To Believe™.

Sara Goggin Young

Sara Goggin Young is an Attorney turned Life Coach and Keynote Speaker, who uses a refreshing and unique combination of mindset, nutrition, and fitness to help you transform into your very best self. Sara has overcome many challenges, including six knee operations, addiction, and divorce, using her Power To Believe™ Toolbox. When Sara learned the tools to change her mindset, fuel her body with premium nutrition, and build strength through fitness, she transformed her own life. She let go of a negative mindset and started crushing her goals, including starting her own business to help others regain their confidence and drive; and achieved a Pan-Am World record, USMS National record, and All-American status in multiple swim competitions. Through her individual coaching, workshops, and retreats, Sara now coaches hundreds to achieve their own excellence every year. Sara's mission is to help you get out of your head, connect with your soul, empower your life AND regain your Power to Believe™ in work, love, and life!

Sara Goggin Young
Sara Goggin Young, LLC
Illinois
708-790-3814
Sara@SaraGogginYoung.com
www.SaraGogginYoung.com

---

5 Ways Overcome Challenges with Strength and Grace

Life is full of challenges, and there is no way around it. My story, like many others, shows using the wrong ways to overcome challenges at first. But, after hiring a life coach and doing the work with their guidance, I learned how to overcome challenges with strength and grace. Here are FIVE ways you can overcome every challenge and empower your life every single time. Shift your low-vibing emotions (anger, anxiety, overwhelm, etc.) into high-vibing emotions (gratitude, passion, love, etc.) My five tools and coaching give you all that you need to get out of your head, connect to your soul, and empower your life.

www.SaraGogginYoung.com/Gift

Sallie Colaco Wagner

*Reclaim Your Life with M*S*G™*

"Sallie, he's gone!"

My mother's voice awakened me.

When I fell into my troubled sleep, I was married. When I woke up, I was a widow. My husband had died.

We had been keeping vigil for a while. We knew the time was close, and now, it had come. He was gone.

There were so many feelings running through my mind and my body.

There was sadness, that he had died.

I had fear about the future.

There was also relief, that he wouldn't need to suffer anymore.

I had so many feelings, I didn't know which one to feel.

So, I mostly felt numb. It was numbness, punctuated by knee-buckling pain and grief.

I also felt guilt.

I fell asleep. Maybe if I hadn't fallen asleep, he wouldn't have died.

Days before, he told me how tired he was. I knew what he was telling me. He was too tired to fight anymore. I told him that it was okay. If he needed to go, he could go. He asked if the children would be okay and if I'd be okay. I lied, and I told him yes, we would be okay.

It was now 4 am on Sunday, and he was gone.

I really felt, and believed, that somehow, I had killed him. If only I hadn't given him permission. If I hadn't told him it was okay, he wouldn't have died. If only I hadn't fallen asleep. If I hadn't fallen asleep, he wouldn't have died.

If only…

Illness

Several years before my husband died, I was diagnosed with fibromyalgia. For some time before the diagnosis, I had suffered from debilitating fatigue. I would spend all weekend in bed, just to be able to function at work during the week.

I experienced brain fog, forgetting things that I had just seen or heard. It affected me at work. One time, I was preparing a financial analysis for a major project that my team was working on. In the time it took me to scroll to the bottom of the spreadsheet — maybe a couple of seconds — I couldn't remember the numbers I had just seen at the top of the spreadsheet.

For me, always priding myself on my exceptional memory, that was devastating.

Of course, there was also the pain. It was constant, never-ending, heavy, aching pain in all my muscles and joints. Imagine that your muscles were made of sand, and the sand was soaked with water. How heavy they would feel and how exhausting it would be to do the simplest thing. It would be very painful to move. That is how it felt to live with fibromyalgia.

That was my life.

I had never heard of fibromyalgia, until my doctor told me I had it. I asked her, "Okay, what do I do about it?" She said, "Live with it."

WHAT??? I didn't know how I could possibly live like that.

I, therefore, tried alternative remedies. I saw a naturopathic doctor. I changed my diet. I took supplements — about a hundred every day! I got injections in my muscles for the pain — 30 or 40 at a time, to the point where I would pass out from all the injections.

I still didn't see any significant improvement. I still had to guard my energy and take care not to inflict more pain on myself.

When my husband's relatives were visiting, we went to the city market to shop and walk around. I carried my purse on my shoulder. The next day, I couldn't move my shoulder because of all the pain. I spent the whole day in bed, totally exhausted.

I was eventually so discouraged, depressed, and debilitated that I felt I couldn't go on. I felt trapped. I felt as if I would have to stay in bed and never leave. I truly believed I would have to leave work and go on disability because I couldn't function any longer.

The worst part was, I didn't see how I could possibly take care of my children.

I was broken.

I then experienced a **MIRACLE!** There's absolutely no other way to describe it. There I was, sick, wondering how much longer I would be able to work. Suddenly, I was healed! I didn't just get a little bit better. I was totally, completely healed!

I have no idea how it happened, except to say that it was a miracle. I didn't change my life, and then I was healed. I had tried all that before, and nothing worked.

No, I was **HEALED,** from the inside, and I changed my life to manifest that healing.

It was as if I had been reborn! I had a new life!

In hindsight, perhaps it was the difference between wanting, and deciding. I had wanted for so long to get better and to have even the slightest bit of improvement. Perhaps something within me finally **DECIDED!** I was healed.

Just five months later, my husband died.

There I was. Devastated again. This time, it was for entirely different reasons.

We were living in Kansas City at the time. My family lived in North Carolina. I had my son and my daughter, and that was it. I wanted to help them through their grief. Yet, I was alone, and grieving, just as they were. Therefore, I didn't have many resources to spare. I was also living with all the guilt, blaming myself for his death and believing that somehow I had killed him.

To make it worse, a woman at work told me how lucky I was that my husband had died.

REALLY???

She explained that at least I knew he was never coming back. In her case, her husband had left her. She lived with the uncertainty, still wondering if he would ever come back.

REALLY???

It's not a contest. One person's grief can't be compared with another person's grief. We can't and shouldn't try to lessen our own grief, by comparing it with somebody else's.

Grief is unique. Each person's grief is their own.

Grief takes its own time.

Mercifully, time passed — you've heard the saying that time heals all wounds.

Let me tell you, that's absolute crap! Time does not heal all wounds. You can put that in the category of things I know now that I wish I'd known then.

Time doesn't heal. How we use time either heals or doesn't heal. When we're purposeful and intentional about healing, we heal. We can't just wait it out.

It was a big mistake on my part.

Nevertheless, time passed. My children and I pieced our lives back together. My kids grew up, and I grew up. They got married, and I got remarried.

Whose Life Are You Living?

Each of us has a story of pain, loss, or change. There are dramatic changes, such as births, deaths, marriages, divorces, job loss/change, and relocations. There are also less dramatic changes. They are no less significant. I call it life creep, when you wake up one day and wonder what happened with your life.

My husband and I were married for almost 23 years. For 23 years, I had known myself in relation to him. Without him, I didn't know who I was anymore.

Truth be told, I didn't know who I was before he died.

For too long, quite possibly for my entire life, I had been living somebody else's life. I was a non-player character in my own life. It was as if my life were planned and ruled by outside forces. I jokingly call them the Alien Overlords.

I spent my time at the shallow end of the pool of life. I skated around the periphery rather than taking center stage. It was because I wasn't being true to myself and the visions of the life that I wanted for myself.

My husband's death put a spotlight on those feelings I had about my life and eventually helped to prompt me to break free of the limitations I had created for myself.

When we're faced with mortality — whether our own or those we love — we start to question our lives.

As I asked those big questions of myself, I realized I was living somebody else's life. I kept asking myself, where did I go wrong? How and when did I get so far off track?

When I was a child, I always wanted to be a teacher. In college, I majored in theology. I started in physics, ended up in metaphysics, and planned to become a professor of theology.

I then met my first husband. The first night we met, he said, you should be a lawyer. Guess what? I'm a lawyer.

I spent my career living somebody else's vision for my life. It looked pretty good on paper, but it felt pretty yucky inside. I was out of place in my own skin, and in the life that was chosen and created for me by the Alien Overlords.

Perhaps that disconnect was manifested, in part, in the fibromyalgia that plagued me. I was healed, yet I squandered my miracle because I just went on with my life, following the path that had been set for me.

Fortunately, life conspired to change all that. Events reconnected me to my earlier vision for my life of being a teacher.

This time, I listened to the message that life was sending me. I recalibrated and focused on teaching opportunities. When I did that, everything changed to the point where I had to scale back. Yet, the universe still wasn't done with me — it never is!

Eventually, perhaps a bit reluctantly, I followed the trail of breadcrumbs that led me to life coaching — becoming a life strategist to guide people to discover the life that makes them come alive. I became a life alchemist to guide people to transform their lives and uncover the magic that lies within them.

It took a while, until I finally listened **again** and answered my calling to live the life that makes me come alive!

It's scary to make that decision and that commitment.

As soon as I did, part of me argued for why I couldn't. It wasn't a good time. It wasn't convenient. I was running multiple businesses already. How could I take on even more?

Another part of me knew that great opportunities never show up when it's convenient or when it's comfortable. Great things occur on the other side of what's comfortable.

I made the decision to let the part of me that wants to come alive and win over the part that's afraid. It was a long journey, yet I still got there. I got here.

I know that there are steps I could have taken that would have accelerated that journey for me. I could have taken the shortcut rather than the scenic route.

That's why I've created a protocol to guide you to create and take your own shortcut. It will save you time and effort and, perhaps, mistakes along the way.

Mind Apps

My life wasn't off track because of Alien Overlords. It was off track because of Mind Apps.

You know what apps do to your phones and other devices. They slow things down, drain the battery, and sometimes have competing purposes.

Mind Apps do the same thing in our lives.

They live in your subconscious mind, which is like your operating system. They're the programming that determines the results you get in your life. That programming competes with itself, and you, for control.

Your Apps likely started out as useful — chunking skills, knowledge, and experience into shortcuts to help you navigate and make sense of the world. For example, you have apps for walking, talking, and driving. They are all incredibly useful.

However, some of your Apps may actually now work against you and what you consciously want in your life. They work in your subconscious mind to sabotage all the wonderful intentions you hold in your conscious mind.

During times of stress, anxiety, worry, and times when we're busy running our lives, careers, and businesses, which seems like pretty much all the time, we run on autopilot. We revert to our default settings, which are our manufacturer's settings.

Those settings tell us what to think and believe about how the world works. The problem is, the things they tell us aren't always true and accurate. That's the crux of it.

You see, it's not what you don't know that holds you back. It's what you do know, that's not true, that holds you back.

So many times, the solution to our challenges is not to learn more or to learn what we don't know. The solution is to un-learn what we know that's not true.

What do you know — that's not true — that's holding you back?

Why do we "know" things that are NOT true?

It's because of Apps from families, society, and the world. They tell us things that are not true, and we believe it. We're constantly bombarded with messages that we have to be a certain way, look a certain way, wear certain clothes, own certain cars, to be worthy and to be loved.

We're told we're too much this, not enough that. All those messages and all that programming holds us back from living the life that makes us come alive.

So how do you reboot your thinking, uninstall those Apps, and install new Apps that allow you to make conscious choices?

The first step to reboot your thinking, is to recognize that everything is a choice.

It is your choice.

When you understand this truth, you can begin the process. Just take the first step and decide.

Ask yourself, do I want it? Or have I decided for it?

Wanting isn't the same as getting. Wanting isn't the same as deciding. Wanting is magical thinking, wishing, and hoping that something will happen. Deciding is wanting plus action. Deciding is wanting something so much, that you take the necessary steps to make sure it happens.

M*S*G™ is your key to deciding and taking the necessary steps to begin the process of defeating the Alien Overlords to reclaim your power over your own life.

M*S*G™ stands for Mindset, Skillset, Get Off Your Asset!

Mindset

Mindset is not just thinking happy thoughts, like Peter Pan.

Mindset is having faith. It is not necessarily religious faith, although it may also be that. It is faith that you will prevail. At the same time, you must be courageous enough to confront the facts of your circumstances, and the reality of what's happening in your life.

It all starts with Mindset.

However, most of the time, we need to take some steps to get the right Mindset.

Skillset

That's where Skillset comes in. Skillset includes new skills and new knowledge of how to change your thinking to have the right Mindset.

One important skill is goal setting. Three guidelines you can use to set your goals are — make it big, ask the right questions, and be specific.

The first goal-setting principle is — make it big!

Are your goals big enough?

Those Mind Apps (those things we know that are not true) show up in subtle ways, especially in the goals we choose for ourselves.

Be generous with yourself in time, money, and in commitment to your own development. It is crucial to value yourself and affirm your worth.

Set big goals.

The second goal-setting principle is to ask the right questions. The quality of your life is determined by the quality of the questions you're willing to ask. It is important to ask the hard questions.

You've heard of the seven levels deep approach. Seven levels are just a start.

Instead of seven levels, think of the process as an infinite onion. You are continuously peeling off layers, in a never-ending quest to get to the core.

Here's the first layer of the onion.

Ask yourself, are you successfully discontent?

Like me, does your life look good on paper yet doesn't feel so good on the inside? It doesn't feel as good as you thought it would or should?

We hide in the questions we don't ask. We allow others to hide in the questions we don't ask. There's no hiding here. You must keep asking questions.

The last goal-setting principle is, be as specific as possible in stating your goals. If you don't specify, the universe will fill in the blanks. You may not get the results you intend. Remember that words matter.

We've all heard about the guy who wishes for a million bucks. He's suddenly surrounded by deer. Don't be like that guy.

Get Off Your Asset!

Okay, you know about Mindset and Skillset. It's now time to get off your Asset!

Once you identify your goals, you're ready to take action.

However, be prepared… what comes next is what stops most people before they get started.

As they start to manifest a new Mindset, they get stopped by fear.

Fear shows up as indecision, distraction, and self-sabotage. Fear is a Mind App, which, as you know, means it can be subtle. It doesn't announce that it's here to keep you from getting the results you want in life.

It sounds like the voice of reason.

It says things like…

How am I going to do that?

I've never done that before.

Now's not a good time.

Should I really be doing this?

I can't do that.

Have you heard those voices, or others?

Don't be the person who is pushed by fear. Allow yourself to be pulled by the vision of the life you're creating for yourself!

It comes down to fear or faith.

You make the choice.

It's all about deciding and making a commitment to and for yourself.

It's that decision and start, which stop most people. So, decide and take action! It is important to use and not just sit on your assets.

Create a System

Now that you've decided on your goals, you're ready to take action by creating a system to move you toward your goals.

The first step in your system is to write your goals down and increase your chances of success to 56%.

The second step in your system is, share your goals with somebody. It can be family, friends, or a goal buddy.

Why don't we share our goals?

Isn't it because we're afraid to fail?

Have you ever failed? Has anybody not failed? Failure is part of the system. It's a tool, not an outcome. It's a resource that you manage, just like all the other resources in your life. When you manage it properly and make it part of your system, you'll find your success.

Take the risk, and share your goals.

When you share your goals and then identify action steps to take toward your goals, you increase your chances of success to 64%.

Those action steps (including the system and structure) are crucial. This is because goals alone won't get you there. Without action steps, your goals are just nice pictures on that vision board you made.

Instead of focusing exclusively on your goals, create a reliable system. It must be something that you can easily, readily, willingly, and happily repeat every day. That's goalsetting to the present. You then succeed every day, not by reaching the goal but by moving in the right direction.

You're already 64% of the way there!

The third step in your system is, make weekly progress reports to your goal buddy. This is the accountability factor. This will increase your chances of success to 76%.

Commitment

All this is the framework and infrastructure you can use to build your own unique system to get the results you want to see in your life.

All it takes is 100% commitment.

Anything less than 100%, even 99.999%, is so hard! It is filled with excuses, and reasons, not to take the steps that will lead to our goals.

100% commitment is so easy! There are no excuses or reasons, just doing. You simply need to follow your system every day. Every day, you should move in the direction of your goals.

It always comes down to reasons or results. You make the choice.

I invite and challenge you. Commit yourself 100%.

You start with M*S*G™.

Mindset — Change your Mindset to one of success.

Skillset — Learn and practice the skills that will move you forward in your success.

Get Off Your Asset, by taking action to bring that success into the landscape of your reality.

You have to take action to achieve your goals.

The right Mindset and Skillset will empower you to take the right action and make that 100% commitment — to you!

So, where are you with your M*S*G™?

Is it (are you) powerful enough to take on the Alien Overlords?

When you answer, "YES!"... you're ready for my 21-day challenge.

First, for 21 days, maintain the Mindset to get the results you want in life.

Second, for 21 days, develop the Skillset to attain and maintain the right Mindset.

Third, for 21 days, take action, by developing a system to move you in the direction of your goals — every day.

Report back to your accountability partner each week and share your results. Report on the mindset that you attained and maintained and the Skillset that you acquired and honed. Report on the system that you developed and repeat every day.

You can then trust that you will begin to get the results you want to see in your life!

Remember, as Ralph Waldo Emerson said, "The only person you are destined to become is the person you decide to be."

Decide for it.

Don't just want it.

Decide for you.

Make that commitment to you.

Reclaim your life with M*S*G™!

Sallie Colaco Wagner

Sallie Wagner is a speaker, author, lawyer, real estate broker and instructor, and Life Alchemist. She is also a hula-hoop enthusiast.

Sallie uses outcome-based techniques, including Emotional Freedom Techniques (EFT), Evolved Neuro-linguistic Programming (eNLP), and trauma-aware modalities. Clients launch into action and gain access to rapid, concrete results, as they ditch those unwanted habits, behaviors, fears, phobias, limiting beliefs and decisions, that keep them from living their best life.

Sallie's continuing mission is to impact lives as she coaches and guides you to fully embrace and integrate the challenges that life brings, in order to discover, create, and live the life that makes you come alive!

Sallie spent the majority of her law career in the corporate world. She co-owns and operates a company that provides broker and contract compliance services to real estate brokerages throughout Florida. She also co-owns and operates a real estate school, providing exceptional educational opportunities for real estate professionals throughout Florida.

A native of North Carolina and long-time resident of Kansas City (Missouri), Sallie finally found the ruby slippers. She currently headquarters in the Tampa Bay Area, Florida, USA.

Sallie Colaco Wagner
Intentional Life Coaching, LLC
Palmetto, FL
816-616-5403
SWagner@SallieWagnerEnterprises.com
SallieWagner.com

M*S*G™ and MORE!

30-day free trial membership of Sallie's Locals community — Sallie Wagner Coaching.

https://SallieWagnerCoaching.Locals.com/support/promo/MSG100

Gladys Santiago

Finding Your Limitless Inner Heroine

I dedicate this story to my Mom, Rafaela "Felin" Santiago (Irizarry-Gonzalez). What would it have been like for her not to die at age 55 and to live three more chapters of life?

Today is July 28, 2021. It is the 25th anniversary of Mom's transition to the gardens of heaven. I am on the island of Vieques, Puerto Rico, captivated by the see-to-the-bottom of the ocean beaches, run-free Paso Fino horses, and grab the smack-in-your-face Big Dipper from the zero-light night sky. This memory I allow rent-free space in my mind.

A testament to overcoming mediocrity is realizing my dream to stay on this offshore island. However, in the spring of 2016, I sat on my couch, caught in a trance in a decrepit apartment outside of Chicago. LIMITLESS was absent on that fateful Sunday when all could have ended. I wish for an eviction of this memory.

I sit here in paradise trying to recall why this God-fearing Christian, bad-ass Latina even pondered ending her life. The sequence of events eludes me, as I chill on the third-story veranda of the bed and breakfast oasis, caressed in glory from the ocean breeze and the dazzling white-light-sun. Still, I remember…

What Happened to Me?

I returned from Puerto Rico in September 2015, after staying three months to be with my Dad for his emergency heart surgery. It was a bittersweet time, indeed a heavy load. I saw the side of him that my Mom had to live with, and possibly the reason why she gave up. I know he was happy that I was there yet contending with his bigger-than-any-elephant-in-a-room mortality. He guarded his troubling health. Not one of his six children knew he was having major health issues! We had become friends over the past 15 years. I shared with him my burdens, and all the while, he held close his (burdens). There we were together, both in turmoil. My Dad passed away on December 31, 2015.

Before I dropped everything to be with Dad, I was headed for rock-bottom.

On January 3, 2015, I was rear-ended on Lakeshore Drive in Chicago, just before "Deadman's Curve." I got out of my car to investigate. At the same time, a tow truck operator had pulled up behind us. He pleaded that we exchange information and get off the road, "I've seen too many highway ricochet incidents."

I went straight to the police station to file a report. The officer noticing my arm twitching, said, "You need to get to the hospital." I went to the emergency room to learn I had whiplash and spasms and was instructed not to drive until resolved.

That morning came to a halt, when I walked into my apartment and dropped to my knees. It was an unconscious reaction, but there I was, at the foot of my bed, thanking and praising Jesus Christ for my having survived the accident. At the time, I did not understand the sequence of events that would ensue.

Unleashed POW!

Life's smackdown had just gotten started. When was it going to stop? I was always struggling, always having to seek justice to inequities from others' blind-spot predictions: female, Puerto Rican, public school-bred, single parent. I was exhausted from fighting these needless battles just to get a slice of the pie promised to me if I graduated from college and even more with a graduate degree. I had both and more. I had succumbed to the vile grip of society's pegged victimhood. This I say in hindsight.

A few months earlier, in 2014, I decided I was done being a fundraising executive and stopped the consultant business I founded in 2004. Something was looming inside. In late 2012, I had decided I could not play second-fiddle, nor did I want to be head of any organization. I recall one executive recruiter's upset. She yelled, "You are one of only a handful of Hispanics with the golden CFRE credential. You are in great demand." From time to time, I would take on a full-time position as a chief development officer with a client organization to help take them to the next level. Those were short-lived. I realized even though I did not want *their* position, *they* could not let go of *their* feeling of inferiority. I am a **Limitless Woman**, and everyone knew it. Everything I touched turned to gold.

Therefore, why did I leave a rich career in philanthropy? A long-time mentor, Dr. Herb Smith, said, "You got tired of the hustle." I suppose that made sense, coupled with being frustrated by clients who did not exercise sound counsel. This was topped by the reality that I brought in millions for others, and here I was making weekly trips to The Salvation Army food bank.

Life was slowly beginning to unleash its whip! In 2014, my financial advisor suggested I become an Uber Driver to bridge resources. I had not heard of ridesharing or discerned my waning from my consultancy. At the time of the 2015 accident, I was enjoying being a 5-Star rated Uber Driver. However, due to the accident, I was ordered not to drive! At least I had a couple of small contracts to see me through recovery. But, around the corner was the next life — POW.

It appeared that everything was imploding at the same time. While in physical therapy, my landlord changed management companies and gave me less than the required time for notice-to-tenant. They announced they would renew my lease for an additional $300 more rent per month! This set me up for eviction! I was facing homelessness, another crisis where I had to fight to defend my rights.

I was at a full stop. I had stopped sourcing consulting contracts, stopped entertaining executive recruiter calls, and was forced to stop driving to heal from my injury. Now, I had to find a new place to live without an income stream.

I did not know at the time that depression caused by accident trauma is both common and debilitating. My life continued to unravel. My attorney was stumped by the callous behavior of the insurance company, even though the girl admitted she was at fault. We only sought what was reasonable. I had to prepare for the long haul as I recovered from neck-pinned stiff, painful muscle spasms.

I knew that the new management company was unjust. I was angry that I had to defend myself once again. I needed to prove that they could not take advantage of this Latina. In researching tenant rights, I found a Jewish foundation that approved my application for rent assistance until I could find a new place to live. I needed to move because I could no longer afford to live in the condo apartment on Lakeshore Drive. At least I was able to check off my bucket list living on LSD. I lived there for five years before being PUSHED out.

The approval of the grant for rent proved my case. The housing court dismissed the case, but I had to pay the court costs. What the hell? Good ole' Chicago hustler's blood was flowing through the judge's veins. Why am I sharing this? Because this predatory, biased, and inequitable behavior and practices is what I have been fighting for most of my life! I have been trying to live a mindset of *Limitless*, but society has not yet caught up with *me*.

Keep in mind that I am ensnared in healing from my injury, defending my tenant rights, not generating income, and about to become homeless. I also do not know what I want to do with the rest of my life. What earnings I made came from Uber driving. It paid for my car loan and insurance, until it did not. I was deep in the rat race, with cats on my tail.

What a difference a year makes. Just fourteen months earlier, I had achieved a weight loss goal, losing 70 lbs. I was generating a six-figure income, had bought a new car, and was able to have my grandchildren visit all expenses paid two to three times per year, including a whole month during summer break. My universe then came crashing down.

If you are still reading my story, you most likely just took a deep breath. You may have had your entire world come down, varying scenarios and degrees, but relative and relevant just the same.

Sometimes Looking into the Past Will Set You Free in the Future

In 2021, almost seven years later, when I decided to participate in the Overcoming Mediocrity book series, I became interested in that which was living rent-free in my memory.

I found three major developments: Depression from accident, childhood induced trauma, and the famous mid-life crisis. I had not recognized any depression or life-shift at the time my world imploded. I was trapped in the vicious cycle of survival.

According to NeuroSpa, TMS Therapy Centers *(March 2020)*, the following are symptoms of mid-life crisis common to both men and women:

- Feeling unfulfilled in life.
- Intense feelings of nostalgia chronic reminiscence about the past.
- Impulsive, often rash actions.
- Dramatic changes in behavior and appearance.
- Marital infidelity or constant thoughts about infidelity.
- Constantly comparing oneself to others, who seem happier or more fulfilled.
- Intense feelings of regret.

Another article shared that "mid-life can be quite tumultuous for women… women are not only dealing with biological changes, but they're also dealing with work problems, family issues, death, securing finances and reaching personal goals." Dr. Susan Albers asks in her article *(Cleveland*

Clinic Women's Health, June 2020), "How do you know it's something deeper rather than a moment of frustration?" You may experience the following signs and symptoms very prevalent to women* in mid-life crisis:

- Depression and anxiety.

- Unhappiness.

- Lack of motivation or desire to put time into certain activities.

- Dissatisfaction with your career and other life choices.

*Men going through midlife crises often feel "trapped" in their lifestyle as they face time's relentless march forward. However, women often experience them during times of transition.

A mid-life crisis is a conflict between a person's perception of themselves and their life as they think they are and what they want to be. It is a desire to change one's identity. A mid-life crisis is a purely psychological disorder, although it can occur as depression. Dr. Albers states, "Depression is a chronic biological-based mood disorder, while a mid-life crisis is not."

Oh no! I saw that what I was going through was "real." After analyzing what was in my control, a *Limitless*-living practice. I saw that I was, in fact, not in control, nor did I realize it at the time.

The research revealed that external situations could aggravate mid-life depression. Oh, let me count the ways: car accident, unjustified eviction, poverty, not being able to have my grandchildren visit, the care and loss of a loved one, and having to sort out Dad's role in Mom's early demise. Then there was menopause. UFF! Women from age 40 — 60 have the highest rates of depression. I will come back to this later, as it relates specifically to Latinas.

The other "major development" unfolding in my life was accident trauma depression. An article in Michiganautolaw.com, *Depression after a Car Accident: What you need to know.* "Depression after a car accident is often both common and debilitating… this condition can take on a life of its own…

this psychological disorder can upend a person's life."

Trauma-induced depression and mid-life crisis were playing ping-pong, and I was the little ball.

Homeward bound. When? Where? Why?

In 2008, I sold my house within a week, cash, top dollar. Equity in hand, I moved to Chicago. It was a dream I had forgotten. I moved in with my kindred-spirit family in the Albany Park neighborhood. I lived there three years, earned my MBA, and realized another dream to live on Lakeshore Drive. However, after the pushout from the LSD condo, I could not go back to my family's house because they had a house full of individuals in transition.

Another kindred sister offered a second-floor "dwelling" in her husband's house in a suburb one hour from Chicago. I accepted, sight unseen. What other choice did I have? What we found (she had never entered the apartment), the previous 27 year-long tenant... NEVER CLEANED THE PLACE! There were urine stains in the carpet, inches of dirt in the windowsills, and a smell that would not go away even after fresh paint. A few weeks later, the orthopedic doctor diagnosed bursitis in my knees and shoulder stemming from the deep cleaning I *had to do* to keep my sanity in this "new" apartment.

Then came the situation with my Dad in Puerto Rico. My mentors, Loling Souder and Samuel Betances, called when they heard about Dad. Loling said, "Glad, Sammy wants to know when you are going to Puerto Rico?"

I replied, "Lo, you know I can't afford to go."

"It's not IF you are going but WHEN Glad. Sammy insists, and he will cover your expenses so that you could be with your Dad."

Their sage wisdom (a priceless gift) knew I would regret not being there for my Dad, and they understood my situation. They know what truly matters, and their generosity is ***Limitless***.

I dropped everything. The look on Dad's face when I entered the hospital room was priceless. As I shared earlier, it was bittersweet. I had no regrets and knew our goodbye would be our last. I cried all the 45 minutes to the airport. Dad passed away three months later, on New Year's Eve.

Back at "home," I continued to heal from the car accident. I was able to drive for short periods and drove for Uber only on the weekends. However, Uber had not caught on in the suburbs. Driving into the city diminished profits and added to my fatigue. I stopped before I did more damage to my body and psyche.

I finally received payment from the insurance company when I was in Puerto Rico. I caught up with a few bills, but that did not matter. My car was repossessed right from under me.

I was never more than 60 days late. I thought I was being responsible by arranging payment online before going to Puerto Rico. Shortly after, one morning, at 4:00 am, I heard a beeping sound. Like most people, I continued sleeping. My car had been repossessed! I called the loan representative, who was just as shocked. He then said, wait for it, "You should not have activated anything online. That is what started the repossession process. You should have continued to communicate with me only." Wait! What? Will I ever get it right?!

Once again, I had to investigate any recourse. I learned that the bank *owed me* for the car! They cut a check for $11K taking the balance owed on the loan — less than $3K. They took away my livelihood. I needed a car to get to and from a new part-time menial retail job, and to make ends meet. I would go into the city to drive for Uber.

I would later read studies that it takes two to three years (longer for women) to recover economically, especially when serving as a caregiver to an ailing parent.

No More Suffering

There I was on that fateful spring morning in 2016, lost in a trance, facing the window. I did not have any answers. I was exhausted and downtrodden.

I did not care anymore! Thoughts of suicide then surfaced. Everything went blank, and blackness surrounded me.

Oh my God! I reached for my power words. "I rebuke you in the name of Jesus Christ!" The morning brightness returned. I sat there, shocked by what had just happened. Mesmerized. How could this happen to *me*? I am a strong spiritual woman. Shame and guilt came over me.

I did not know what I did not know about the one-two-three-four and five punch of accident and childhood trauma-induced depression, mid-life, no livelihood, and grieving Dad.

I decided to turn on the TV. Joel Osteen was on. His message is my mantra today. Jesus Christ did not abandon me. He continues to be my ONLY constant. I learned weeks earlier that the house was going to be sold and demolished. As you can see in the photo, with a marker in hand and the wall as my canvas, I wrote: "**Anchored to Hope….**"

 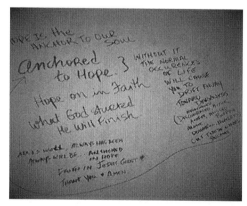

Hope Lets You Dream Again

Enough of the dark. I cannot live in that space anymore. It almost killed me. I chose God again on that fateful morning; peaceful, quiet confidence ignited my *Limitless Inner Heroine*.

I have only recently begun to share with others about that day. I kept facing limits and kept finding the way through with the help from the Bible, meditation, exercise, and a few trusted friends. You cannot hide from the hard parts of life. All you can do is find the people who will support you through it.

Essential to my lifeline has been a tribe of kindred spirits. Acts of love and kindness flowed: a kindred brother loaned me his car, a kindred sister sent me two checks totaling $15,000, and my Dominican Sisters and Associates of Peace stood by me in retreat. They understood that my soul was knocking. My cousins asked me to join their triathlon and cover the swim portion, my first personal best. A friend showed up unexpectedly to help move me back to Chicago. Another dear friend called asking for my guidance, as she began her journey through the mid-life *rite of passage* (versus crisis). God sent her so that I could understand for whom I was going through all of this.

When the student is ready, the teacher will appear. I decided to complete reading the Bible. I had only to read the last few books of the New Testament. I learned those were mostly written by St. Paul. The lesson from St. Paul: My tragedy is not unique in human history. I laughed at myself. Who was I to think I had the patent on suffering? God has equipped me with *Limitless* strength needed to overcome every obstacle.

A dear friend said to me, "When you keep heart and mind on God, you can suffer gracefully and in joy." I added, "I can play from my soul."

God's Summons

During one meditation, I was asked to contemplate on what I really wanted. At once, I stood up and said out loud, "I want to go home." I did not have an attachment to a particular place. God did. A few days later, Loling called, "Glad, it's time for you to come home." Deep sigh.

Hope is the sense that grace can happen. You never know what is around the corner.

One day while driving from an event with Sammy, he shared how people were talking about me, perceiving me. I was shocked and hurt. Then he said, "I told all of them. I will *never* give up on Gladys!" I burst into tears.

A couple of days later, during one of our dominoes playing (counseling) sessions, he said, "You have a unique set of experiences and competencies that can transform Latinas. I would like you to write a book on "Igniting the Potential of Latina Single Moms.""

I pushed back, "Why? There are already books written on the subject."

He said, "Really? Turn on the computer next to you and look up Latina single moms."

I thought that I would prove him wrong. I sat down and typed in… Latina… single… moms. About three books appeared, along with ten porn sites. I sat up straight, eyes opened wide, my mouth dropped, and my breathing began to tighten. Then I remembered Sammy was sitting next to me. I noticed his reaction from the corner of my eye. I do not believe he expected it but he was happy to see my reaction.

I turned in his direction, looking him in the eyes, and said, "What the hell is this? There are millions of books written about business. How dare I limit the number of books for Latinas? What do I have to do?"

He has coached me for a while on the process. I have been engrossed in thinking I had to do it myself, but I am done with *me, myself, and I*! While they are beautiful, they alone will not deliver the message to Latinas that they are Light in the world.

Doing the research for the book, I learned that the unhealthiest demographic entering mid-life are Hispanic women, especially if they are single mothers. I also learned that mid-life is when women are prone to let diseases take over. ***This cannot be sustained***. Mom was going through mid-life. She died of breast cancer. Stricken with fear, she ignored her body, signaling her to "Wake Up!" I recently forgave myself for thinking, "Dad, killed Mom," based on my experience with him in 2015. I have forgiven Dad (and Mom) for the violence in our home that may have driven Mom to give up. She did not know what I now know and continue to discern. Forgiveness sets us free.

In January 2021, I returned to my hometown, Cleveland, Ohio. God continues to send me kindred-spirits who are aligned with my promise: *Latinas are equipped to transition smoothly through three more chapters of their life.* We are creating ***The Latina Illumination Center***.

Good or bad, nothing in life stays the same. We simply accept, embrace and absorb that Hope remains forever.

Gladys Santiago

"Unleashed Vitality, Now and Forever" is Gladys' promise for the world. She is the Founder and Owner of Unitivity, Inc., bringing 30 years of strategic visioning and stewardship to deliver excellence to her client's vision and mission.

In 2008, Gladys secured the CFRE credential from Certified Fundraising Executive International. In 2010, she earned an MBA in Entrepreneurship and Managing Innovation — Summa cum Laude (Illinois). Twenty years earlier, she earned her BA in marketing and economics from Baldwin-Wallace College (Ohio).

She is certified in Diversity Intelligence and a Certified Volunteer Administrator. She is a graduate of Landmark Education's Curriculum for Living Program, The Wisdom Global Power and Contribution Program, and

The Team, Management, and Leadership Program. She served as a Coach in the LE International Discourse Project.

Gladys is an Order of Preacher Associate of the Dominican Sisters of Peace. She is a multi-medium artist and a Latina single parent of proud blended heritage children.

In 2021, Gladys returned to her hometown after living in Chicago for 13 years. She was born and raised in Cleveland, Ohio, of Puerto Rican descent. She is bilingual in English and Spanish. She is the first in her family to graduate from college. She was the First Latina school board member for the Cleveland Municipal School District and representative on the National Council of Great City Schools. She completed two fellowships with The Broad Institute for School Boards on school system reform.

Gladys is an effective leader and has served on numerous boards. Her work and volunteer experience include design and execution of strategic plans, conferences, programs, and events resulting in record-breaking fundraising; increased public and private partnerships; recognition of corporate volunteerism; award-winning parental engagement; recognition of "Hispanic Women of the Year;" and, facilitated hundreds of individuals completing leadership development programs.

Are you living a life from innate gift(s)? If you have the will to thrive, Gladys will help Ignite Your Light!

Gladys Santiago, CFRE, MBA, OPA
Unitivity, Inc.
Cleveland, OH
773-551-9593
GladVitality@gmail.com
www.UnleashedVitality.com

Your Light, Your Purpose, Your Journey

To stop the automatic way of life takes a deliberate act. This gift is yours to look at eight areas in your life where you may want to bring consciousness (the state of being awake, aware, and responsive). Congratulations on self-generating Your Light, Your Purpose, Your Journey.

https://OvercomingMediocrity.org/gladys-gift

Julia Hsia

The Perfect Journey

*"Loving Ourselves Through The Process of Owning Our Story
Is the Bravest Thing We Will Ever Do."*

—Brené Brown

We all have secrets that we hold close to our hearts that take great courage and vulnerability to share.

If we only knew the limitless power that can be unleashed WHEN WE DO.

I am the black sheep of my family — a rebel, without a cause. Growing up, we had a room with ta-ta-mi flooring (the traditional Japanese bamboo mats). This room is where my mom would send me for timeouts. Inside, above the door, hung a black and white picture of my Dad.

"去反省 Qù fǎnxǐng Go kneel in front of your dad and reflect," she would tell me. Like Bart's writing on the chalkboard from the animated sitcom, *The Simpsons*, "I will not…"; I spent a lot of time reciting "I will not…."

The funny thing about getting in trouble is that I would always get caught. ALWAYS!

Prelude

Sophomore year. School had just started. I was already feeling overwhelmed: body image, getting attention, being liked, the usual. Every day, the school bus I took snaked around the vast apartment complex and made stops at different buildings. After dropping me off at the last stop, I walked to our building at the very back of the complex, up to unit #205, our one-bedroom apartment on the 2nd floor, dragging my feet the whole way.

It was a little after 3 p.m. Baba (Dad) was getting ready to go to his second job. During the day, he worked at Kmart collecting carts and was an office janitor at night. Mom was also home. She had just moved from Taiwan to live with us permanently. After three years without mom, we finally had her back. However, it wasn't how we expected it to be.

I walked past the living room that also served as my Dad and brother's bedroom and into the bedroom Mama (Mom), and I shared. It was a small, cramped space that felt like a prison cell. Mom was sitting on the bed. Her hair was uncombed, her eyes were puffy, and her skin was dull. It was very different from the working mom look we were used to seeing her in. Next to her was a stack of auto sections from the newspaper.

"Yun, call about these cars for me," mom said, calling me by my Chinese name. I glanced at the stack of ads blanketed with red circles. Mom needed a car. However, I just got out of school. I was tired. I was sixteen. The last thing I wanted to do was make phone calls to a car dealership. The flood of self-doubts swept over me: my English was not good enough for me to have a conversation. What if they said something that I didn't understand? What would they think of me???

She handed me the phone. I threw it back like a reflex, aiming at no place in particular. The phone bounced off something and fell on the bed. It did not land on the wall behind mom. Instead, it hit her head, right by her hairline and above her eyes. The blood started pouring out and down the side of her face. My throat tightened, and I immediately ran to her and began to sob and apologize. Just a few minutes later, there was a knock on our door. It was the cops. Neighbors heard the screaming and crying and had called 911.

The ambulance showed up shortly after. The officers told me which hospital they were taking her to. Through my tears, I murmured, "Mama, 對不起 Duìbùqǐ (I'm sorry)… We will meet you there, Baba and me." Mom was calm this whole time. She comforted me, "Don't cry, it will be OK. We cannot let them know this is something you did." Before taking her in the ambulance, she instructed, "Do not tell them what happened. I hit my head on the corner of the kitchen cabinet. That's what you tell them. Yun, you have to change your temper. *You have to change.*"

Made in Taiwan

I am a product of pure love. My Dad was Chinese literature and history teacher in Taiwan. My last name 夏 Hsia (sh-a) means summer. 夏老師 Hsia laoshi was what students and the locals called my Dad, *teacher Hsia.*

Dad was a peaceful man, and his students enjoyed spending time learning from him. My mom was among Hsia Laoshi's fan club. The bond strengthened between them, and the friendship blossomed. A few years after my mom graduated, they got married and started a family. My mom's family did not welcome their union due to the age difference, and my Dad was from China. The common perception of the Taiwanese people is that 外省人 Wi-shen-ren (person from the outer state) are outsiders and cannot be trusted.

Mom and Dad lived a quiet and simple life in a small housing unit assigned to teachers. I was born in the summer of 1970 and was named 昀 Yun, which means *light*. I was loved and doted over. There were many pictures of me. I smiled and laughed everywhere: on the couch, next to the birdcage, and in mom and Dad's arms. Life was so full of joy.

This peaceful lifestyle abruptly stopped when two men showed up at the little housing unit and took my Dad in for questioning for his political stance. Someone had turned in a list of communist suspects, and my Dad's name was on the list. My Dad did not come home that day, the next day, or the day after. He did not come home until eight years later, when I was ten. The year was 1972, and my younger brother was yet to take his first breath outside of our mother's womb.

Whatever It Takes

Life was challenging without Dad. However, help was always available to get us through the hard times. We needed a new home as the school was tearing down the smaller housing units in which we lived. The widow of the high school principal learned about Dad's misfortune and donated her housing unit to us.

On a very windy day, we moved from the very back of the row to the very front. We had spacious rooms and a large yard with flowers and trees. We even had a bomb shelter. The school's basketball court and sports field were just on the other side of the fence. I remember hearing students cheering 加油 jia-yo!, 加油 jia-yo (*fuel up*), during volleyball and basketball games and the soothing sounds of flutes echoing through the campus during my late afternoon naps.

Without Dad's teacher salary, mom got a job. She worked as a teller at a bank across the street from our grade school. I remember watching her practice riding her scooter, going around the school's track at night. *Whatever it takes.* I learned this philosophy from mom, and it has served me well.

My brother and I were independent, first-generation latchkey kids. We walked ourselves to the public bus stop to and from school. Mom would take me on her scooter when I was running late, which was often. She would sometimes even have both my brother and me on the back of her scooter.

She was and still is a *super mom.* She taught us how to use the rice cooker and do chores, such as sweeping and cleaning dishes. We did not have much, but she always made sure we had books to read. One new book a month was my reward for doing chores. At night, after we went to bed, mom studied and passed multiple tests to advance her career. Although our family's financial situation improved, the hard-working discipline was instilled deep within my brother and me. We take nothing for granted.

After eight years, Dad was released from prison. The four of us were reunited for the first time in our home. We were a typical family, just like the others. FINALLY!

Dad took over the kitchen duties and helped us with our homework. He taught us how to ride our bikes. One of my fondest memories is him waking me up at 6 a.m. to ride our bikes to the fairground to jog and do group exercises. I often did not want to get out of bed. Dad would patiently check in every few minutes poke my arm with his fingers until I got up. After working out, we would bring breakfast (soy milk and fried greasy sticks) home for mom and my brother.

Dad being a scholar, education was always the fundamental part of our upbringing. Mama and Baba recognized whenever there was a learning opportunity. We frequently went to used book stores for old books and magazines. Dad taught us Chinese literature, and we recited poems. He also taught us English, and there would be mock tests to make sure we were paying attention.

This peaceful honeymoon stage did not last. Dad could not find a job. Fights between my parents broke out regularly. Mom did most of the talking. Dad would just listen silently, then ride his bike and disappear for hours. Sometimes he would take my brother and me. We would ride our bikes to the beach, where we collected seashells and played with the tiny crabs in the sand.

One of Dad's sisters lived in Chicago. Dad confided in her often through letters about our family's hard times. "Why don't you apply for immigration? It would be a better future for everyone," Gu-gu (auntie) suggested. Going to the land of opportunities and starting fresh would be good for everyone. There are plenty of jobs, and the educational environment is much more open and relaxed.

Our application kept getting turned down because of Dad's criminal record. Who would want a communist in their country? We remained hopeful. Then one day, it was approved! A letter from my uncle's senator friend gave us the green light to enter America. We've done it!

Coming to America

The long-awaited day finally came. Mom had gone through our belongings for months and carefully selected the essential items to bring: clothing, books, and cookware, such as steamers and woks. We did not know there was a Chinatown where you could buy all these things.

We loaded up eight oversized pieces of luggage into the van that my uncle (mom's younger brother) borrowed and drove up to the Taiwan International Airport in Taoyuan. It was late at night, and my uncle brought a friend along to help share driving duties, since it was going to take eight hours.

One of my godsisters, er-jiejie (second sister), had stopped by to wish us well. I had a new crisp white shirt with 龍 long (*dragon*) on the front. Mom purchased this and the dark green Capri jeans specifically for me to wear on this special day. The shirt was just a little too big and too long. Er-jiejie took off her belt and put it around my waist. Just like that, the clumsy-looking shirt became a fashion statement. Little did I know that this would be the last time we saw each other. A motorcycle accident ended her life. I cherish this lasting memory of her.

On a rainy September day in 1984, we arrived at the Chicago O'Hare International Airport with eight pieces of luggage. It was a different country, a new beginning, and a chance to start over.

New Beginnings

Mom went back to Taiwan after a month to return to her duties at the bank, since she remained the breadwinner of our family. But not without finding a home for us to live in first. I still remember the excitement and joy she had when she shared with us about the one-bedroom apartment she had found. She set us up with everything we needed, including a green shower curtain to match the green bathtub and an old used car for Dad. Then on a cold November day, we drove Mama back to O'Hare and said our good-bye through tears.

Dad worked two jobs to provide food and a roof for my brother and me. He never complained. We were in survival mode. Luckily, my brother and I could help out. My cousin's Chinese restaurant was hiring! My brother and I started our restaurant careers washing dishes and cleaning tables. We saved up our money and pitched in to buy a better car for Dad. We settled on a used Buick Century.

Dad loved that car. Every Sunday, he would take his bucket filled with tools, put on his gloves, and go out to the parking lot to check the oil and tire pressure. I also got to enjoy this 8-cylinder beauty. I learned how to drive in this car. It escorted my brother and me to numerous rock concerts and the college orientation at Illinois State University. Behind the wheel, I could go wherever I wanted and experience the freedom that I seldom felt I had. I have been in love with driving ever since.

Americanize Me

Starting over in a new country to me meant turning my back on my roots. I wanted to speak better English so that I could be accepted. Wanting nothing to do with my Chinese heritage, I spent a lot of time at the library reading and learning. The books and magazines helped me gain insights into the American culture. I also spent a lot of time watching TV, particularly sitcoms. SNL and movies, such as Stripes and Tootsie, were major influences on my sense of humor. I secretly wanted to be funny like Bill and brave like Dorothy.

By 1987, when I was a sophomore in high school, Mama resigned from the bank and moved here from Taiwan. We were a family once again. However, I was not the little girl that she remembered and resisted everything she had to say. "What does she know? She just came here. I have been doing just fine," was the song I was singing in my head. I also started to drink alcohol at my cousin's restaurant: a little bit of rum here and vodka there. The older waitresses sometimes would sneak me into clubs to drink and dance with them. I thought that was very glamourous and fun. I could not wait to be 21, so I could buy my own alcohol and go to bars!

The American Eagle is White

By the summer of 1989, I had successfully molded myself into a cool American teen who drank and even occasionally smoked. We loaded up a friend's van with coolers full of alcohol on a beautiful summer day and headed up to Great America.

The van started to have problems, not even a quarter of the way there. I started drinking right out of the Southern Comfort bottle because I was bored. The sweet whiskey had a bite, but it went down very quickly. We decided to turn around. By the time we got to my friend's house, I had passed out, cold, leaving the half-emptied bottle of Southern Comfort.

After throwing up all over my friend's house, I was able to make it back to the one-bedroom apartment where my family lived. It was very late at night, and I had not called to let anyone know where I was.

Mom was still up and was in the living room. She immediately commented on the smell I emitted. It was not pleasant, a mixture of vomit and alcohol. My brother came out of the bedroom that he shared with my Dad, wanting to know what happened. "Go make her some tea first," mom said to my brother, affixing her eyes on my pale face.

"We went up to Great America," I proceeded to tell my made-up story, "But the van broke down on the way back. We waited until my friend's father came to pick us up." Mom and my brother did not buy it. I can't blame them. It did not make sense. That, plus the fact that I am the worst liar, didn't help.

"So you went to Great America?" my brother inquired, "What color is the American Eagle?"

Heck, I don't know, I thought. Quick, pick a color. Black, eagles, are black, aren't they?

"Black," I confidently answered.

"Black? You went to Great America and saw the black American Eagle?" My brother drilled more.

I stared back at him, knowing what was coming next.

"It's white," he said quietly, "It goes around the whole park. You can't miss it."

Caught again.

Bowl of Rice

With the help of government grants and loans, I attended college. The original plan was to study physics then transfer to an engineering program in a more prestigious school. The higher power had a different plan for me.

In my Sophomore year, I registered for lithography 101. It was 50 percent out of interest and 50 percent out of convenience. My dorm was on the outskirt of campus, and every class was at least a 15-minute walk away except for the Turner, which was the Industrial Technology Building. Graphic Communication was one of the sequences under this category. I declared this as my major and continued taking classes in the printing lab.

A regular day in the lab involved working with the camera and developing film in the darkroom. There was also a single-color printing press for students to learn the printing process. Learning this trade not only provided me with the skills to produce visual communication, but it also enhanced values, such as patience, that my parents have demonstrated and instilled in me.

During the second semester of my Senior year, I was offered an internship with a leading printing company in Chicago. This comprehensive program allowed me to work with each of the six sister companies, and I really gained an insight into the printing process from beginning to finish. This valuable experience resulted in a job offer one week before graduation. I found my first bowl of rice!

Chinese culture compares getting a job to having a bowl of rice. There is no rice nor a bowl when we are still in school. We have to search for a job to get the bowl and then fill the bowl up with rice. If you can find a good match, even though it may not be the perfect job, it's still better than nothing at all.

To keep from starving to death, we need that bowl of rice. In the event that we get fired, then that is called losing the bowl of rice 丢了飯碗 (Diūle fàn wǎn).

Although I was content with my bowl of rice, I wanted to have the ability to create my own bowl. Having witnessed my Dad losing his teaching career and the sacrifices that mom made with her career, I wanted to have the freedom to have my own financial independence. I started taking business classes, freelancing, and tutoring Chinese outside of work. This was the beginning of my entrepreneurial journey.

Silent Illumination

After finding my bowl of rice and buying a house, getting married was next on the agenda to complete my American Dream. Both of which I did. In 1997, I bought my first home and married my high school crush in 1999.

Having two bowls of rice, I now lived a life of stability. "Look at me. I'm just like everyone else now!" But at the same time, deep down, I still yearning to be accepted. The insecurity of being an outsider continued to create an imbalance within me.

Like mom instructed, I told no one about what happened in our apartment on that September day. The secret was filed away, just like the family secret of Dad's jail time.

I was happy and joyful on the outside but unfulfilled and unsatisfied on the inside. My complex of shame, fear, and anger continued to develop. Something was not right, but I did not dare to take action. It was as if there was a noise in the car, and you turned up the radio to drown it out. I was living a life of denial.

Searching for ways to fill the void inside, I shopped and consumed. I would find myself wandering around the store with a coupon, looking for things to buy, even if it wasn't something I needed.

My mom kept a watchful eye on my life and knew I was in a downward spiral. To save her daughter, she suggested that all of us to attend a meditation workshop together. After the workshop, I became a volunteer at the temple and attended the workshop every Sunday morning. Then one day, my Dharma teacher asked if I would be interested in being the treasurer for the temple. "Sure," I accepted with gratitude. I've never been selected for a leadership position. I was honored.

Connecting with the Buddhist community was life-changing for my family and me. When Dad passed away in 2004, the community came to our home and chanted with us to provide closure for his 80-year journey.

Along with reflection, meditation provided a cleansing method for the mind. Dust began to settle, and I started gaining a sense of self-worth. I was given more responsibilities at the temple, including serving as the emcee in fundraising events and leading study groups. Instead of chasing and wanting to be like others, I was comfortable being Yun.

Attitude of Gratitude

One does not always see where the relationship will take us at the beginning of the journey. Life comes full circle when the timing is right, and all the chips fall in place.

In 2009, the economy collapsed, and I lost my bowl of rice. I could not be happier. I had wanted to start my own marketing business for years. In fact, I invested in software and registered the company name Reflection Communications, LLC, with the state, just weeks before the layoff.

A friend connected me with Dynamic Professional Women's Network, DPWN, a local referral group looking to fill all categories for the new chapter it was launching. This is where I first met Christie Ruffino, the founder. Through Christie, I learned about Toastmasters, a public speaking club she belonged to. I joined and became a member right away. I continue to serve as a club officer to the present day, carrying on the club mission by offering a positive learning environment to help others develop communication, leadership skills, self-confidence, and personal growth. It was also Christie's invitation to this co-authoring program that led me to the opportunity to share my story.

I am a life learner, and life is full of precious opportunities to practice. After 20 years of laughs and tears, my marriage dissolved peacefully. After breaking my mom's heart over and over, I am now making her proud as 夏老師 Hsia laoshi (teacher Hsia).

My bowl of rice continues to be filled with different grains of rice: an entrepreneur, a teacher, and now, an author! This would not have happened if not for the causes and conditions that were made long ago, and I am so grateful. I am grateful for the sacrifices my parents made, the support and love of everyone that I have connected with, and the challenges that were put on my path to guide and inspire me.

My purpose is to honor my loved ones with our story. Most importantly, I am here to share the power of reflection and the limitless potential that we all possess. I am here to embrace our vulnerability with confidence, welcome our sufferings with gratitude and celebrate our differences with compassion.

"You have to change, Yun," were mom's words, as she was being taken to the hospital years ago. I kept my promise. No longer ashamed, I now fully embrace who I am and let my light shine.

And now I'm going to help you do the same.

Love yourself. Own your story. Believe in the journey.

There is nothing like the power of reflection. It is limitless.

Julia Hsia

Julia is a Chinese American from Taiwan, who has been living in a Chicago suburb since 1984. A wrongfully accused and convicted sentence of her father's political stance resulted in her family's choice to make the journey to the United States. This family secret resulted in a full set of limiting beliefs, including a sense of shame which impacted her creativity, self-expression, and way of connecting and communicating with the world as well as with herself. Her transformation began when she learned the power of reflection.

With this shift of mindset, she is now able to call forth the alignment, cooperation, and partnership of others. She is living the limitless life created by design. After graduating from Illinois State University with a B.S. in Print Communication, she started her career as a digital production artist. In 2009, she founded Reflection Communications to assist businesses with multi-channel marketing communication. In addition to being the founder of

Reflection Communications, LLC, she is also the Chinese Mandarin host of One Kind Moment Podcast, a Chinese language teacher with students ranging from Chicago to Atlanta, and a seasoned Toastmaster member who has served multiple clubs and was recognized as the President of The Year in 2021.

Her hobbies include beekeeping, improv performing, drumming, and tap dancing. She is a lover of nature and spends time hiking in the woods with her loving Pitbull companion Frank.

Julia Hsia

Reflection Communications

3833 E. Main Street #1048

St. Charles, IL 60174

312-865-0245

Limitless@ReflectionCommunications.com

ReflectionCommunications.com

Free 5-Day Challenge to Overcome Your Limiting Beliefs

Internal limiting beliefs usually come from personal experiences. They can hold you back and keep you from achieving your limitless potential. In this challenge, you will learn how to develop a reflection method so that the illusions from your past will no longer bound you.

Take this free 5-day challenge to start living unlimited TODAY!

https://ReflectionCommunications.com/courses/limitlessliving/

Dr. Jamie Thomure

Finding My Passion by
Getting to the Root Cause

What if I told you there was a condition that seven million women in the United States suffered from, but only half of them knew that they had it? That is 10% of all reproductive-aged women! I would be willing to bet good money that many of you who are reading this have never even heard of it either.

This condition is Polycystic Ovarian Syndrome (PCOS). What is PCOS? It is a hormonal imbalance in which the ovaries produce too much testosterone and other androgens. If you have PCOS, you might have ONE or MORE of the following symptoms: irregular periods, weight gain (especially around the middle), difficulty losing weight, acne, hair loss on the head, hair growth in a male pattern (face, back, etc.), difficulty getting pregnant, mood swings, depression, anxiety, sugar cravings and more.

The most common conventional "treatment" for PCOS is to take birth control to "regulate hormones," which sometimes masks the symptoms but doesn't get to the root of WHY a person is having these symptoms. Rather than simply masking the symptoms, I LOVE to help women figure out what is actually driving their PCOS and how to work WITH their body to balance their hormones and end the frustrating symptoms.

My story is all about how I came to do this work that I love to do. For many women, their story is clear. It was one big event that changed the trajectory of their lives forever. That is not my story. I have come to what I do now, by a lifetime of miniature nudges and insights from the universe. While my story might not flow in a linear way, these are the details that led me to where I am today. I couldn't be more excited about it!

Grandpa's House

Growing up, my grandpa was one of my favorite people. He was quite the jokester and was always trying to pull a fast one on me. My family went to his house on weekends. He always made me feel like the most special girl in the world (other than my sister, who I'd like to think was a close second).

One evening, as we were preparing dinner, my grandfather started acting funny. He was pale and seemed shaky. His words were slurred and didn't seem to make sense. I didn't know why my grandpa, who was always so strong, was acting so strange. It was scary!

My grandma ran over to the refrigerator, grabbed the orange juice, and poured him a cup. A few minutes later, grandpa was back to his normal self. "What happened?" I asked. I knew my grandpa was a type one diabetic, but I had never known what that meant. My parents explained that his blood sugar got too low, and he needed to eat. However, to me, it all seemed mysterious. While I didn't quite understand what I had seen, I never forgot the impact that my grandfather's blood sugar had on him.

I later learned that my other grandfather was a type 2 diabetic. Having these two men in my life with similar issues created a curiosity in me, which led me to PAY ATTENTION every time blood sugar was mentioned. This curiosity continued through high school, college, and eventually through my chiropractic education.

The fact that my parents, myself, or my sister could have a genetic predisposition to diabetes further motivated me to dive into this topic. What I found was astounding!

Weight Gain with A Side Of Acne

People joke about the freshman 15. However, for me, it was no joke. I gained about 15 pounds and began to suffer from severe acne. It was a really frustrating time, since I didn't understand what was going on in my body.

I began dieting, reducing my calories, and recording everything that I ate and drank… for my entire senior year. I added my activities. I rounded up on the food calories, in case my portions were bigger than I thought. I made sure to have a 500 calorie deficit each day, so that I would have a 3500 calorie deficit by the end of each week.

Using the energy balance equation that I learned in my coursework, this was supposed to result in a slow, steady one pound/week weight loss. Guess what… IT DIDN'T WORK! By the end of my senior year, I was the heaviest I had ever been. And my acne was no better.

At one point, I was put on birth control for the acne… you know, to "balance" my hormones. Now that I know more about what was really going on, I shake my head at my younger self and all those who were guiding me. There was no way that the birth control pills would ever get to the root of my issues. They only would mask my symptoms, while bringing a whole other set of side effects, like mood changes and more weight gain. I couldn't get to the root of the problems just yet, but I would soon.

It's Not Just Calories

Just after graduating from chiropractic school in 2010, with a strong desire to continue learning, I signed up for a seminar series on the "Anti-inflammatory Diet." The speaker, Dr. David Seaman, was amazing. He had done more research than anyone I had encountered up to this point, and he was challenging all the traditional views of weight loss and nutrition.

After telling us what the anti-inflammatory diet was, he went into the research. One by one, he linked common conditions to inflammation. He explained how the Standard American Diet (SAD) leads to inflammation, which contributes to all of the conditions, such as diabetes, arthritis, cancer, skin conditions like acne and eczema, neurological conditions like depression and anxiety, autoimmune conditions, hormonal imbalances, and more.

Wow, his explanation blew my mind! I began to wonder if there was more to my acne and weight gain than simply counting calories. As a doctor, I have found that I am my best guinea pig. I'm leery of advising my patients of something I have not done myself. So, I got right to it. I switched my diet, getting rid of processed food and adding more veggies. Guess what? I lost those 15 pounds, and my acne cleared up. In addition to these benefits, I was surprised to realize that I wasn't experiencing the seasonal allergies that were a part of my life every fall!

For years after this seminar series, I LOVED helping others to improve their diet, by eating real food. However, I wanted to dive deeper. As helpful as food is, I knew that there was more to health than just eating well. I took a year-long functional medicine training program, which trained me to get to the ROOT CAUSE of WHY a person has certain symptoms, rather than simply prescribing a medication based on the symptoms.

This course only fueled my desire to learn more about how to heal the body, rather than simply treating the symptoms. Over the next few years, I read all sorts of books and listened to podcasts, anything I could do to learn more. Every time I was in the car, folding laundry, or doing dishes, I was listening to something to help me learn more.

Getting To The Root Of The Issue

The more I learned about functional medicine, the more I wanted to help EVERYONE! Keeping this knowledge to myself just wasn't an option. I talked my patients' ears off during their chiropractic adjustments, but I never had enough time to get my whole message across.

Since this happened repeatedly, I realized that I needed to find a better way to share my message. Eventually, I knew that I wanted to create a course! With a course, I could teach people all of the information and work with people from anywhere and everywhere! The potential was LIMITLESS!

However, who should the course be for? All of my colleagues stressed the importance of specializing in ONE thing... So, I thought about myself. What did I need when I was struggling with weight and acne? Instead of focusing on calories or masking the symptoms with birth control, getting to the ROOT CAUSE and BALANCING my hormones was what I needed. When I understood what was driving my weight gain and acne... I found the solutions to fix it!

I decided that I would help others in the same boat. They wanted to get to the root of their problems, not just mask the symptoms. I focused on helping anyone like me who could use a real food diet and a root cause approach to take control of their symptoms. Then I met Sarah, Jessica, Julie, and Chris.

What Is Possible Once You Know Your ROOT CAUSE
(Names have been changed to protect privacy)

Sarah's Insulin

Sarah was a beautiful young lady, who wanted to become pregnant. When she was unable to conceive on her own, she turned to her doctor for advice. Her doctor recommended weight loss. But HOW? She had tried dieting, and it never worked. She could stick with it for a few days or weeks but would always fall off the wagon. In addition to her weight, her menstrual cycles were irregular, and she suffered from acne.

When we started working together, I explained how her insulin was a driving factor for not only her weight but her acne and her irregular cycles! She was open to trying a new path to weight loss that might help her in her attempts to conceive. I introduced her to a way of eating that supported steady, healthy insulin levels.

When she began eating this diet, her cravings went away. She was able to stick with it. She ended up losing 50 pounds! Her acne improved, and her periods were regular for the first time in her life! And best of all, she became pregnant with a healthy and beautiful baby girl!

Jessica's Stress

Jessica and her husband had been married for about three years, when they decided it was time to try for a baby. She went off birth control, but her period didn't come back. As we talked, her story came out.

When did she start taking birth control? Age 18. Why was it prescribed? It was because her period had stopped, when she joined the high school cross country team.

Jessica was still an avid runner. She did marathons and ran about 60 miles/week. She loved to clip coupons and could fill her refrigerator for about $30-40/week. She was mentally stressed about not having a period.

It became apparent that the amount of exercise was causing too much stress on her body. Her diet was too low in calories for her exercise level. The processed foods that she was eating were causing inflammation in her body.

We had a long conversation about nutrients. We explored why her period stopped in the first place. We discussed how pills that were intended to "balance her hormones" were simply masking the deeper issues. She thought that she was getting a "period" each month while on birth control, but I explained that because the pills were blocking her from ovulating, that this was merely a breakthrough bleed and not a real period. In my experience, with most people, when the body is fully nourished, ovulation and real periods return.

As we explored whether her body had the nutrients needed to have her reproductive system functioning, she recognized that eating inflammatory foods wasn't helping her. She went from being an expert coupon clipper at the grocery store (which got her lots of "food" for a low price, but also a cart full of processed foods) to jumping on the anti-inflammatory diet bandwagon with a focus on getting as many nutrients as possible!

We modified her exercise regimen to something that was a lot less stressful on her body. She added meditation and more activities that brought her JOY into her daily routine!

When she did this, she actually GAINED about 20 pounds. However, that was what her body needed to balance her hormones. Even as a nutrition major in college, she didn't realize that her body had been underfed and undernourished. It took about a year, but her period came back! She was able to become pregnant and now has three beautiful children!

Julie's Inflammation

Julie was looking for a change. Her cycles were irregular, and she suffered from alternating constipation and diarrhea. She wanted to lose weight. Her doctor also told her that her triglycerides and her cholesterol were too high. This was enough motivation to modify her lifestyle, if only she knew what to do.

Together we got curious about what her symptoms were telling us. We discovered that she had some insulin resistance, but inflammation was one of her main drivers. Nobody had ever explained to her that digestion issues could actually cause her hormones to become imbalanced!

We put her on an anti-inflammatory diet and a gentle gut healing protocol. Over the next several months, she lost 30 pounds. Better than that, her cycles became regular and MUCH less painful. Her energy increased. The next time she had lab work done, her doctor was impressed at the shift in both her triglycerides and her cholesterol!

Chris' Thyroid

Chris came to me in a lot of pain. She had been diagnosed with PolyCystic Ovary Syndrome (PCOS), fibromyalgia, and hypothyroid. Her energy was low. Her sex drive was non-existent. She felt bloated constantly. Her mood was low. Her cycles were all over the place, and she wanted to lose weight.

Even though she was taking thyroid medication, her symptoms indicated that her thyroid was still unbalanced. In addition to her thyroid, she had issues with both insulin and inflammation. She was ready for anything, if it would free her from some of these terrible symptoms.

We began working with a real food diet designed to address the root causes of her symptoms. We were delighted when she began to feel better. Her energy increased, while her pain decreased dramatically. Her cycles began to regulate, her pain and energy levels improved, and she started to lose some weight.

Then one day, she called me concerned that her anxiety was getting worse. She felt like her heart was beating out of her chest. I recommended that she call her doctor, who manages her thyroid medication, to run some tests.

It turns out that once she was eating a better diet and her gut health improved, she started absorbing her nutrients better. This led to a better conversion of inactive thyroid hormone to active thyroid hormone. It also resulted in better absorption of her medication. Her anxiety meant that what we were doing worked. Her hormones were balancing themselves, and she no longer needed the same dose of her medication!

PCOS A Surprising Connection

I hear stories every day about women who are struggling. They don't feel comfortable in their own bodies. They have tried taking various medications, cutting their calories, and exercising more, but nothing has worked. Many of these women are surprised to find out that they have something called PolyCystic Ovary Syndrome (PCOS).

So many women NEED This message!

Whether you are struggling with your insulin-like Sarah, your stress levels like Jessica, inflammation like Julie, or thyroid like Chris. *There is hope for you!*

I LOVE to help women figure out what is actually driving their PCOS and how to work WITH their bodies to balance their hormones and end the frustrating symptoms. For far too long, traditional medicine has left these women without answers, leaving them to suffer needlessly.

That course I mentioned earlier was created specifically to address the needs of women with PCOS symptoms. It was named BALANCED because that is the vision… balancing your hormones and bringing lasting balance to your life.

If you have struggled with something similar, I want to empower you to find the root cause! Your body wants to be HEALTHY and VIBRANT, and understanding how to best work with your hormones will put you on the path to get there.

I do what I do because of women like you. I LOVE hearing your stories, showing you what is possible, and seeing the TRANSFORMATION! The possibilities are LIMITLESS!

Dr. Jamie

*If this resonates with you, I'd like to invite you to take my free BALANCED online workshop. When you sign up, you will be given access to a ROOT CAUSE quiz developed just for women like you. Let it be my gift to you! You can register for this online class at our website www.DupageFamilyWellness.com.

Dr. Jamie Thomure

Dr. Jamie has a passion for helping people get to the root of their health issues. Believing in the body's ability to heal when given the proper support, she teaches clients how natural methods and lifestyle changes can impact the body.

Jamie is the owner of DuPage Family Wellness, a chiropractic office in Warrenville, IL. While she loves seeing patients in her office, she desires to help even more people. In an attempt to do so, she has created two online courses: "7 Weeks of Real Food" and "Balanced."

In "Seven Weeks of Real Food," people explore how eating "real food" can be life-changing. Participants are encouraged to make changes to their eating habits, as they learn the "why" behind the recommendations.

"Balanced" is a program designed for women with PCOS who want to lose weight without just eating less and exercising more. Throughout six months, these women learn what is driving their symptoms and how to balance their hormones through natural lifestyle changes and supplements.

These courses help women to get to the root cause of their issues through small achievable steps. Rather than a one-size-fits-all approach, women discover which lifestyle changes would be most helpful for them to feel their best. They are also invited into an online community, where they can find the accountability and support they need to be successful.

In her spare time, Jamie loves cooking, growing veggies, reading, spending time in nature, and of course, hanging out with her husband and three daughters.

More information about these courses can be found at her website below.

Dr. Jamie Thomure D.C.
DuPage Family Wellness P.C.
28W530 Batavia Road
Warrenville, IL 60555
630-448-0255
DupageFamilyWellness@Gmail.com
www.DupageFamilyWellness.com
www.Instagram.com/DupageFamilyWellness

BALANCED Webinar and Root Cause quiz

This webinar will give you access to the first three steps of our BALANCED method to help you find the root cause of your hormonal imbalance and finally lose weight (and get rid of your other annoying PCOS symptoms). We will also give you our root cause quiz, so that you can learn for yourself which root causes might be contributing to your hormonal imbalance.

www.DupageFamilyWellness.com/Class/Free-PCOS-Webinar

Therese R. Nicklas

Finding Joy by Discovering Your Life's Purpose

"Do what brings you joy and your purpose will unfold."

—Iyanla Vanzant

Do you know your life's purpose? Everyone is born with a purpose. It's where your unique talent waits to be expressed. When you discover your purpose, life's magic appears. It is that tranquil feeling of being in flow. Joy and success manifest when you live your life's purpose.

Here's the good news — finding your purpose is your birthright. My paternal grandmother lived her purpose. It took me many years to appreciate how her grit, resilience, and wisdom helped her stay on purpose and helped me find my soul.

It was 1956. My arrival into this world was dicey. Born eight weeks early and weighing 3 pounds, my parents were told I had a slim chance of living 24 hours. And, if by some miracle I survived, I had a strong chance of having to endure multiple health challenges. A premature birth was pretty much a death sentence when I was born. This news didn't sit well with my paternal grandmother. Upon hearing of my diagnosis, Nonnie said to my father, "Take me to my granddaughter." When she arrived at my bedside (a crude version of a NICU incubator), she lifted me up, held me, and said to my dad in her native Sicilian, "If you give her my mother's name, she will watch over her." My father quickly approached the hospital chaplain and asked him to christen me on the spot. So with my grandmother as the witness, I was given my great-grandmother and grandmother's names — Teresa Rosalia. Eight weeks and many prayers later, I was released from the hospital, weighing a whopping 5 pounds. Defying all the odds, I miraculously left the NICU with a clean bill of health and a bond with my Nonnie that even death couldn't break. One filled with unconditional love, profound life lessons, and a winding road toward finding my life's purpose.

As a little girl, I spent Sunday mornings with Nonnie. While standing at her elbow, I learned how to make meatballs, pasta, bake bread and sew. As much fun as it was to cook and sew with her, the best part of our time together was hearing stories of her life as a young girl, her family in Sicily, and why she and Grandpa left Sicily for a better life. It was her life's mission and purpose to enjoy the limitless opportunity of financial freedom.

My grandmother arrived in Boston in January 1928, where my grandfather established a home for his 21-year-old bride and baby boy. Leaving Sicily, family, and everything familiar was a huge risk. Nonnie's no-limits mindset gave her confidence that America was her ticket out of poverty. Where most saw obstacles, Nonnie saw an opportunity. My Nonnie used to tell me, "If you can work with your hands, you will never be hungry." This was her way of expressing the importance of being self-sufficient — a value that was fundamental to her life's purpose.

Nonnie had no formal education. She had gut instincts and a clear purpose. When Grandpa proposed, she said "yes" with two conditions — "Take me to America, and let me handle the money." It was unusual for a married woman to have so much control at that time. Although Nonnie was a quiet, gentle soul, she had a gift for leading with a gentle hand. Tiny in stature — barely 4 feet 10 inches tall, she was dynamic. She was empowered by knowing her value — brilliant, determined, and wise.

Nonnie was generous, while squeezing a quarter until it cried. She shared openly about how she handled money when there wasn't much to manage. She did it conversationally, as if she was sharing her favorite recipe. Money was a tool. It wasn't emotional. It just was. Every night, Grandpa would come in from the barbershop and put his black velvet money pouch on the table. Nonnie would meticulously count out the coins and combine them with what she earned, mending and washing laundry. Their income was divided into envelopes — rent, food, utilities, savings, and, no matter what, charity. Giving to charity was Nonnie's way of blessing her "abundanza" — showing gratitude for having the ability to create more than enough. She was my greatest teacher and the most successful woman I've known. Nonnie's four children were raised on her positive money mindset and abundance mentality. Sadly, only one followed her path.

At 14, I got a job working in my uncle's beauty shop. Working for my dad's younger brother was delightful. He treated me with kindness, respect, and appreciation. It was a joy to work with him. He was by far my best boss ever. He respected the fact that I had two years prior experience working in my dad's salon. My uncle also paid me three times what my father gave me! Now, if you asked my father about his brother and money, dad would snarkly say, "He has the first buck he ever earned." My uncle was unphased by the opinion of others. Like my Nonnie, he found it easy to talk about money. During our commute to work, he would ask, "So, little Teresa (his pet name for me), what are you doing with all the money you're earning?" I wasn't offended or surprised by his query. His approach was so much like his mother's that I felt very comfortable answering. "I'm saving to go to Greece with school next year," I'd proudly reply. "Make sure you keep a little for your pocket. That way, you won't feel deprived and be tempted to do something stupid with your money," he'd advise. My second money sage was my uncle — what a blessing to receive his money perspective!

I couldn't have money conversations at home. Money was always a source of contention and stress. My parents fought over money all the time. Their arguments always made me uncomfortable. I had no idea until much later that knowing how to talk openly about money would help define my life's purpose. Knowing how to speak openly about money builds confidence to ask for what you deserve in all areas of your life. Asking for what you need is an essential key to building your net worth.

It was 1994. I was a young wife and mother of two little boys. My husband's business was evaporating due to the recession. We knew we had to do something significant to improve our financial future, but what? We knew instinctively that we were on the wrong path, but what was the right one? After many conversations, often waking up in the middle of the night, we decided Gerry should go back to school to finish his master's degree.

I had an identical job description to one other co-worker. It was a typical payday, and the department manager made the rounds, leaving our paystubs on our desks. I remember opening my stub and nearly jumped out of my chair with excitement. "Wow, I got a raise!" I thought to myself. I was beyond thrilled. With Gerry in school, money was pretty tight. I did some quick math and realized my new income would be enough to cover our household expenses without adding to our debt.

I was about to call him with the news. My joy was quickly shattered, when I turned the pay stub over and saw it wasn't mine. My heart dropped. The check belonged to my co-worker, the one who shared my job description. I remember feeling so frustrated and angry. In a state of shock and disbelief, I remember thinking, "We have the same job. Why is he paid more?"

That night, I had the most vivid, lifelike dream. Nonnie was singing "Happy Birthday" in her thick Sicilian accent. Along with the special serenade, she repeated the story of the day she held me for the first time. That powerful dream changed my life. She passed away 15 years earlier. However, as if by magic, I was transported back in time, enveloped in her unconditional love. I remember thinking, "If you were here, Nonnie, what advice would you give me?" "Ask" was her answer.

With the dream fresh in my mind's eye and Nonnie's voice in my head, I mustered the courage to confront my manager. He clumsily explained that my co-worker earned more because he had a bachelor's degree. I mentioned that it wasn't a job requirement. He refused to budge. A degree wasn't required for the job, but excellent written communication in English was essential. We were writing sales proposals. English was my colleague's third language. His writing skills were below company standards, and I had to re-write many of his assignments. He earned 20% more than me (the person that redid his work) because he had something our employer found valuable.

Knowing how to talk about money gave me the courage to confront my manager. Not getting my desired outcome taught me that, like Nonnie's desire for a better life, if anything was going to change, it was up to me to change it. I have to take 100% responsibility for my life. My dream of Nonnie reminded me that I was given the gift of a normal, healthy life. There must be a plan for me. What is it? What is my purpose?

This experience was the cattle prod I needed to eliminate what held me back from getting a better-paying job — a four-year degree. With my husband in grad school, how could I go to school at the same time? I had no idea how I'd make that happen. So, like Nonnie, I looked for the opportunity in the obstacle and learned my company offered tuition reimbursement as a benefit. Now that cost wasn't an issue, I had to make it work with my schedule. To qualify for tuition reimbursement, I had to work full-time and maintain a 3.0 GPA. Luckily, I found an evening program designed for adult learners. I enrolled immediately. Twenty-two months later, after going to school nights, working days, while raising two young boys, I graduated magna cum laude.

Earning a degree opened doors that were previously nailed shut. My income nearly doubled shortly after graduation. However, something was still missing. It was great to earn more money, but I felt depleted. My search continued for that "perfect fit" where income, inspiration, and joy meet. My soul yearned for work that gave my life *meaning, purpose, and joy.*

Ah, Joy! The inner GPS to being on purpose. Tired of the grind of soul-sucking work, I thought becoming my own boss was the answer. Since I come from a long line of entrepreneurs, I took a leap of faith, jumping into the empty pool known as self-employment!

By following my metaphorical yellow brick road, I landed on the doorstep of the last place I expected to call home — investments and financial planning. Like Dorothy in *The Wizard of Oz*, I had to pass many lions, tigers, bears (and a few witches) to get to my Emerald City. Most of the time, I traveled alone. In 2021, I found my "Glinda the Good Witch" and realized the answer to my burning question was inside me all along.

For almost two decades, I've helped women create bright financial futures. Intuitively, I knew my wealth coaching system wasn't enough for permanent transformation. After completing the Canfield Success Principles™ Coaching Certification, I discovered what was missing — joy. By combining Success Principles™ with wealth coaching, "True Wealth Coaching" manifested.

The first step toward lasting transformation is knowing what makes your heart sing and fills you with joy. By living your purpose, you create "True Wealth" — a life filled with joy and what money can't buy. My purpose is to help others find their life's purpose and experience "True Wealth" — a life they love that's filled with joy.

Like Dorothy, I needed a coach to help me discover my purpose, find joy and create true wealth. Nonnie created "True Wealth" by living her purpose. She was a limitless woman who continues to inspire me.

Therese R. Nicklas

Therese R. Nicklas is a Certified Financial Planner™, Certified Money Coach(CMC)®, and Certified Success Principles™ Coach. She specializes in helping executive women who are at a crossroads and feel uncertain about their next steps. By empowering them with smart money strategies, they learn how to build their new big, bold life with certainty, clarity, and confidence. She is passionate about inspiring women to enjoy their best life by coaching them toward creating the means for a life of meaning. "Money is a tool to design your life in a way that makes you feel alive and fulfilled. True wealth — true financial freedom — is being free to focus on the things that matter most to you in life — the things money can't buy."

Her distinctive coaching system — True Wealth Coaching™ helps draw the answers you need from you to create a life you love. You'll get clear on what you want from life — and the steps you need to take to attain your goals.

"Traditional Financial Planning merely scratches the surface. Creating a life you love takes more than knowing your net worth. You need to know at a deep level what makes your heart sing and fills you with joy. When you lead with joy and purpose, you discover true wealth — the things money can't buy."

Nicklas is the President and Founder of The Wealth Coach for Women, Inc. She's the author of *"The Money & Life Playbook — 5 Simple Steps To Get Control of Your Money"* and the online course "Six Weeks To Financial Freedom." She has been a featured guest on many podcasts and contributor for major publications. When she's not helping clients transform their lives by discovering their purpose and creating more joy, she's following her passions — exploring the world, playing with her grandchildren, spending time with friends, family, and her rescue dog Gracie. Her motto is "live your life by design and not by default."

Therese R. Nicklas, CFP, CMC, Certified Success Principles Coach
The Wealth Coach for Women Inc.
800 Hingham Street
Rockland, MA 02370
781-413-1090
TNicklas@WealthCoachforWomen.net
https://WealthCoachforWomen.net

The Shortest Path to Success
Dissolve the Emotional Blocks Standing in the Way of Your Best Life

Knowing your life's purpose is the shortest path to success. When you know with clarity and certainty what you are meant to do, work seems effortless, and success naturally follows. Women seek my help because something is in the way of their happiness. They say they feel disconnected, and the work they're doing is sucking the soul, life, and joy out of them. This course is designed to help you break free from what's been holding you back from showing up fully as your best self — so you can finally achieve your big goals and make the leap from where you are to where you want to be.

https://MoneyMasteryMovement.com/Courses/Success

Jennifer Neal

Just Because I Can, Doesn't Mean I Should

Initially, I felt like I had been punched in the gut. Where had ten years gone? Why wasn't I successful in achieving my dreams?

While it took a few years for me to truly identify as an entrepreneur, I had embraced the lifestyle and the vision. I also expected that after ten years, I would be sitting on the beach enjoying that laptop lifestyle.

When my assistant came into my office one summer afternoon and remarked, almost casually, that Formula Done had been in business officially for ten years, it was as if those entrepreneurial dreams popped and vanished into thin air.

The Problem

I needed to get down to the core of WHY I felt so gutted. Over the course of the next few weeks, I spent time working to identify what the problem was and the possible solutions.

For ten years, I successfully ran a digital marketing agency, building everything from simple websites to complex funnels, automated follow-up systems, and membership sites. I helped create and launch six and seven-figure programs, built online courses, and developed the systems that launched many other companies to success.

While creating success for others was entertaining and fulfilling, I had my own dreams that deserved attention. I was no longer going to let anything or anyone (including myself) get in my way. Although scary, coming to this conclusion made me feel powerful.

New Found Confidence

For the first five to six years that Formula Done was in existence, I doubled my revenue each year. I got certified with tech companies, and the referrals they sent me and client referrals kept my business growing without any advertising.

After some time, I even hired and certified additional people to work for me. We were a boutique agency providing top-level white-glove services for our clients, easily building off of my 20 years of experience in the corporate world. It was AMAZING! Everything was going great... until it wasn't.

The Downfall

My business didn't double again. And again, the next year. I blamed it on running an agency. It was simply too difficult to scale. Right? WRONG! When I looked at the situation, I realized that I was breaking one of the cardinal rules I preached to my customers.

I was trying to do too much. With each new customer, I was essentially designing a new business from scratch. I didn't have repeatable systems. We took on work that we weren't experts in, which meant I had to learn new skills to implement. It was great for our customers — they could throw anything at us, and we delivered. However, it was terrible for a business model.

Just Because I Can, Doesn't Mean I Should

I finally realized that just because I was a technical person, didn't mean that I should be building my business around it. Just because I can, doesn't mean I should.

I still have a hard time with that statement. It took me a lot of processing to even be able to say it. However, it took even longer to actually run my business following that mantra.

I knew I had to define my niche and clearly define a product — that was how I would scale past the income cap. I was convinced that the agency services we provided were already niched down, and we couldn't remove anything else from our list of services. Therefore, the key to creating a niche product was in creating a new product.

At first, I jumped on board with an actual physical product. For some reason, I decided that the key would be becoming an Amazon retailer. I had extensive experience with it, and I didn't see a point in straying from what I already knew. That would be a bit crazy, right?

The Charger Catastrophe

During my time of searching for answers, I joined different group coaching programs. In doing so, I met many successful people selling products on Amazon. I decided that was it — my ticket to scaling!

I bought into an Amazon sellers' course and learned all of the ins and outs of the business. After doing all of my research, I landed on buying... wait for it... phone chargers.

Yes, I said it. Phone chargers! I created a new DBA and a new custom brand. I set up my storefront and my new listing and ordered 500 chargers.

Our chargers sold pretty consistently on Amazon, but it turns out that becoming a retail seller isn't all it's cracked up to be. It was like having a second whole business. After a while, it became too much to handle, on top of maintaining sales and fulfillment in my agency.

So, we closed up shop. To this day, I have over 300 chargers in storage, hoping to find another good use for them.

The lesson? Again. Just because I can, doesn't mean I should.

The Niche Nightmare

For so long, I'd convinced myself that I had a specific, specialized, niched down agency. It only took me about a year and a half to realize that I did NOT, in fact, have a specialized niched down agency. I'd been lying to myself all along out of fear.

Pride took over for a while, as I struggled SO HARD to cut things out.

We were really good at everything we did! So, who do I turn away?

I started to convince myself that I liked doing certain things again, thinking, "Well, I like doing this — it's fun again! Ooh! Or maybe I should do this!"

And there it was like a stake in the back... that fear that what if I was saying no to the wrong thing. I had been trying to pivot for years now, and I really felt I couldn't afford another mistake.

The terror gripped me every time I started to close in on an opportunity. I would get that jolt of hope — maybe this is the thing. My mind would fast forward to what that success looked like. And then... the FOMO kicked in and would destroy me.

I tried different things. Should I sell a different package? Would I even still be happy doing this? I spent WAY too much time contemplating. One of my coaches told me that it was time to plant my flag and say THIS is what I want to be known for.

In order to put my name, experience, time, and energy into ONE thing, I wanted to KNOW that I was starting from the right place. Which, for me, meant going back to the numbers — because I can always trust the data.

The Research Project

The first thing I did was to make a list of past customers, their lifetime value, and the types of projects we did for them. I sat down with my team, and one by one, we ranked each customer on a scale of 1-5.

For each one, we ranked how profitable each project was, how much we enjoyed working with them and how much we enjoyed working on the project.

I took the most successful businesses that ranked highest for us and looked for patterns in what made them successful, trying to find a common thread. What I found wasn't really a surprise. It all came down to content — messaging — and exposure.

Repurposing

One of the projects that we identified as a winner was content repurposing for social media. When we had done that project, I thought that was a brilliant idea — I mean, how hard would it be to repurpose content and publish it on social media?

Come to find out — it's hard, really hard! In fact, I tried and failed three times before creating a system that let us repeat the process easily. Once I had it mastered, I created a course and hired a Facebook ads agency to run ads for me.

It worked!! I sold nearly 200 students into our social content machine program! It was awesome!

Except

However, while I made just over $12k in this process, I had spent nearly $50k with the ads agency. They said it was normal and that I should expect to make up the money with another program that I upsold.

I was completely deflated. In order to make money, I had to not only spend a ton of money but also create and sell another program! I had to find another way — one that didn't cost so much.

The Google Juice

Enter my friend, who is a professional blogger. She gets TONS of traffic for FREE!

This must be the new ticket! If I could find a way to repurpose content and create organic traffic, then that $12k would be all mine!

I went back to work to figure out how to create quality SEO content, by repurposing existing content. Why? It allows digital marketers to use blog traffic strategies without having to become a blogger. It also made sense for social media.

As it turns out, people don't want to invest in something that they won't get an immediate return on. There had to be a way to get more free traffic with an immediate return on investment.

Therefore, re-enter paid ads. I didn't want to hire another agency because I didn't agree with the way they run cold traffic expecting conversions. However, when I looked at how social platforms like to control traffic and really study how content marketing works, I discovered the hybrid agency secret.

The point of being all over social media is to get exposure. That exposure should direct new eyeballs to your offer — but no one wants to be sold immediately. They want to get to know you first. I, therefore, sat down and started brainstorming.

At this point, I was committed and determined to create a formula that would work for everyone. It would be a way to make money without the need to keep upselling, while keeping ad costs down. That is EXACTLY what I did.

The Organic Leads Machine

What I created was a model that uses the best of paid traffic and SEO blogging techniques. The result Is the Organic Leads Machine.

More leads for at least half of the traditional ad agency cost. It was insane and amazing!

I had finally found the key... again! I'd created a course that would teach the premise of how to set up the formula for each person's individual business. It was their own personal Organic Leads Machine. I actually enjoyed beta testing, working out kinks, getting real-time feedback, and starting to actually sell my new product.

It turns out that most people want to either just have it done for you or want to have these methods taught to their team. I've come to realize that this is completely fine — and totally doable (and fulfilling)!

Full Circle

I am now doing consulting to help more established businesses customize this model and train their internal team on how to implement and repeat the process.

A full three years later, Formula Done is back in agency mode.

It turns out that I don't hate running an agency. I just needed to niche down, focus on one thing and do it well.

It feels like I've heard that before somewhere.

However, I have many more plans on deck — including teaching other agencies how to do exactly what I'm doing and avoid the agency burnout.

For now, I'm happy sitting in my little leads niche here, running an Organic Leads Machine and helping other businesses to be successful. All the while, I am enjoying also seeing my dreams come true. I have my product. I have my niche. I have a business that scales. It just took me a bit to get here

Finally — my laptop and a beach are not so far off!

Jennifer Neal

Jennifer (Jenn) Neal is the CEO and Founder of Formula Done, tech geek, marketing expert, wife, and Formula 1 racing fan all bunched up into one!

Jenn's extensive qualifications, paired with her magnetic, bold personality, has attracted an array of driven business owners to see her as their reluctant hero. Jenn worked in corporate, small business marketing for nearly 20 years, before running her own digital marketing company for 10+ years. She was frustrated with trading time for money and building other people's dreams. Jenn decided it was time to make her own dreams a reality. She worked hard to reinvent her business and successfully relaunched her agency, Formula Done (formerly known as Kane and Associates, LLC). She's since converted from an operator of her business to a successful entrepreneur.

Jenn worked hard in her business and, over time, identified the patterns that worked (and the ones that didn't) for the companies she'd previously worked for. She'd realized that the key was content and consistency. She knew that it is crucial to have the right CORE system in place to attract, direct, and retain the traffic once you find it.

Jenn has developed, tested, and successfully launched products in and around content repurposing using her own method called Content Activation. She is now a well-known authority on traffic, content repurposing, and messaging.

Jenn loves being on stage and sharing her knowledge with the world. Given her ability to understand complex information, Jenn is an expert who loves to translate "geek talk" into information that anyone can understand. She is a valued business owner with a dedicated staff who enjoy working with her. Jenn is known to encourage her staff to think outside of the box and share their ideas with confidence.

Jenn is a leader in the market and knows the roadmap to online success. She believes that small businesses are the key to strong communities and not only give back but create an upward growth cycle. Being a strong, influential entrepreneur herself, Jenn believes that entrepreneurs can change the world for the better through strength and determination.

Jenn currently resides in Boise, Idaho, and has an insatiable thirst for life. She's an adventurer who loves to travel, certified scuba diver, dedicated wife, a car fanatic, animal lover, and HUGE Formula 1 racing fan, whose favorite color is purple.

Jennifer Neal

Formula Done

10400 W Overland Road #310

Boise, ID 83709

208-780-0400

support@formuladone.com

FormulaDone.com

The Content Activation Masterclass

Generate leads and traffic online using the content you have already created.

Inside This Masterclass, You'll Learn:

- Six Marketing Trends You Can't Ignore — And how to use them to attract and sell to the people most likely to buy from you

- The Content Repurposing Framework — Six Steps to boost your online omnipresence factor and save time

- Hands-Free Content Activation — The secret to creating your content cash machine

- The Five Profit-Killing and Time Sucking Mistakes — Keeping experienced entrepreneurs from Online Success

https://links.TheVirtualJenn.com/6my6

Josephine Moran

The Cost of Financial Freedom

Financial freedom means many different things to different people. By definition, it means you have enough financial resources to cover your living expenses and allow you to afford many of your life's goals. Freedom implies that you are in control of your finances and life choices. For many people, life choices often affect your control of your financial freedom. The ability to clearly see where choice and control intersect on your life's financial journey to freedom is the key, and often the most elusive, as I will share my personal life's journey to claiming and fighting for my financial freedom.

I grew up in a home of humble means. My parents came from the generation of hard workers. They spent only what was needed and saved the rest. Both worked, and my childhood was happy, even though I did not have much. My parents made the most of what we had, and that was good enough for us. We were taught that education was extremely important and it would change our lives. Since neither of my parents went to college, they did everything they could to ensure that their three children did. We all did very well in school and went on to college. I chose my profession to be in the fashion industry and graduated cum laude from the Fashion Institute of Technology with a B.S. in Marketing and Management.

Life-Changing Realization

There were several very pivotal moments in my life that changed my trajectory and moved me toward the experiences I was meant to have. I was 28 when I got married and soon after that got pregnant. It was not by design, but I was grateful to start being a mother. I was in the retail fashion business making a decent salary, and my husband drove a truck for Fed-Ex. I was the breadwinner, and we got by. However, it was far from a comfortable lifestyle. Fast forward, married now with a toddler and very concerned about finances and the future, I read a book entitled "Buy Term, Invest the Difference" by David Babbel. The concept was buy term life insurance instead of whole life insurance, invest the difference in what you would pay for your whole life, and if disciplined, your financial future would improve. I was fascinated, intrigued, obsessed, and filled with passion. That day, I decided to change my career to the world of financial services. Not long after that, I was accepted into the University of New Haven to obtain a master's degree in Finance and Financial Services. My new journey had begun.

While working for a direct sales company, I realized that I had a gift for sales. I became the number one salesperson for three consecutive years. During that time, I obtained my life and health insurance license and sold long-term care insurance for GE Capital, my first true financial services position. I then had the opportunity to work for a new home financing and construction company, where I learned all about credit and became the top salesperson in the company. Unfortunately, after three years, that company went out of business. I found myself looking for another position in the financial services industry. I stumbled upon an ad that caught my eye — "If you have sales experience, understand credit, and want to become licensed, we are looking for you." It was a Financial Specialist position offered by First Union Bank. I applied for the position, interviewed a few days later, and was offered the position within hours. My career in banking had begun.

Home and Career

It was 1999. I now had two young boys. I was going to school at night to obtain my master's and started my new banking career. When I met my ex-husband, he actually knew very little about some of the most basic life skills needed to manage through life. He did not even know how to write out a check. That should have been my first clue. Did this make me think twice? Of course not. I was going to help him. I was going to be his savior. I would take the lead and responsibility and take care of both of us. Things began to get a bit more challenging, as my husband was also beginning to drink heavily, which was becoming a serious issue. He never missed a day of work. He was also a loving, attentive father, which probably made me justify that his drinking was not serious. However, he was really a child himself. He did not think of his job as a career. It was only a paycheck. He did not truly understand financial or adult responsibilities.

Looking back, it is easy to see how his family upbringing brought on many of his issues and lack of real-life understanding. Nonetheless, we were in love. I was going to be a limitless woman and take care of everything. I was always an overachiever who, by most accounts, was successful. When I set my mind on something, I got it, regardless of the challenges. I could handle my husband's flaws and fix him, or at least that is what I thought. It was a major burden for a young woman just beginning her life journey. Over the years of our marriage, I had to overcome many obstacles to avoid financial hardships due to bad choices of relying on him or his family to make grown-up decisions. This included paying for my first pregnancy out of my pocket because my husband's employer (his father) excluded pregnancy coverage to reduce his premiums. My husband and I were on his plan. I also had to pay for an attorney for my husband's DUI, by selling my jewelry because he refused to sell his motorcycle to cover the cost. I started to work several jobs to allow us to purchase a house, while he did little to contribute. However, I was determined to be successful in my career, provide well for my family, and have it all. I still had that feeling of nobility. I could still save him and his family, and of course, that feeling of guilt and obligation.

My career flourished at First Union, then Wachovia. I did extremely well and worked my way up the corporate ladder. I never lost the passion for making a difference in people's lives and continued that mantra as a leader. I graduated from the University of New Haven with a master's degree in Finance and Financial Services in 2002, which opened even more doors for me at my organization. Things seemed to actually get better for a bit. My husband began working two jobs, which kept him very busy and productive. I then received a significant promotion, which was more money but was also going to be even more demanding of my time. We had three children who were involved in a variety of activities that required parental guidance and attentiveness. We had very little help and were paying significantly for childcare. We decided that it would be best for the children for him to work part-time and attend their extracurricular activities, assist with carpooling and playdates, cook dinner and perform projects around the house. It seemed like the right thing to do. I continued to provide for the family. He would provide more time to the children. It eased my guilt to think that my children would be with their father, not outside caregivers. The intent was the right one. Unfortunately, this was the beginning of the end.

About a year later, I got a promotional opportunity for one of the most coveted positions in the bank. The position was in New Jersey, next to where my wonderful parents lived. However, my husband's part-time schedule and family duties were not working for him and us. He now had more free time, which led to more drinking. I thought a fresh start in another state, away from his drinking buddies and with help from family, would make a big difference. I also thought it would help ease my guilt, that constant battle of having to provide for my family but not being around enough for my children, especially as their mother.

I had my dream job. I was able to buy my dream house in a very nice suburban neighborhood. I was also finally near my family. I solved things. Things could only get better, or so I thought...

The Moment of Truth

Fast forward to February 17, 2010. It was Ash Wednesday. Driving home after having attended a very stressful meeting at Wells Fargo, I called the house and spoke to my husband. Something was not right. He did not sound like himself. I had a sick feeling in my stomach. What would I be walking into when I got home? My plan was to take my three children to church that evening to attend Ash Wednesday mass, as we did every year. He was supposed to be cooking dinner and ensuring that our three children were ready to leave when I arrived. My worse fears were affirmed, when I walked in. He was slouched over the stove with his eyes barely open, speaking in slurred speech, highly intoxicated. I gathered the children and whisked them off to mass. Arriving just in time to attend the ceremony, I sat next to my daughter, age seven, hugged her, and began kissing her hand. The pit in my stomach became even bigger, when I smelled alcohol all over her fingers.

I waited until mass was over and in the car to speak to her about it. She told me, "Daddy keeps a brown paper bag in the truck and reaches back to take sips while he drives." He had spilled beer on her while driving. My mind raced. I was overcome with many emotions, including anger, guilt, self-pity, and sadness. Did I ignore all the signs that pointed to this moment? His drinking had gotten out of control. He was now endangering the children. Further conversations with the boys confirmed this, and other very disturbing behaviors were revealed. What had I done? Was this my fault? Had I been that blind to think the children wouldn't be impacted by his behavior? I decided that day that he had to leave, and I had to move on. I had stayed with him because of the children and, by doing so, had created a dangerous situation for them. He was out the next day. Unfortunately, it didn't last long. My guilt allowed him back into our lives with the promise that he would change...

The Shield of Invincibility

My career continued to blossom throughout this time. I received many awards and accolades. I was touted as a highly regarded leader in the financial industry. I persevered in making a difference for people, teammates, direct reports, peers, and clients. However, was I making a difference for my children? Was the fight for financial freedom worth it? I continued to struggle with my guilt and my family obligation, although I tried to spend every spare second with my children. This was becoming increasingly difficult with my new job's demands. Continuing to carry the entire responsibility of the household, the finances, the children's education, and their welfare was making it impossible to balance work and home life. I was a prominent leader at work. I had to play the part, be in control, be positive and lead the team to success. No one had any idea what I was dealing with behind closed doors. I was the epitome of having it all, career, handsome husband, happy marriage, lovely children, and having it all together. Being a role model to others was important. I did not want to let anyone down. I was always myself and never phony. However, I never displayed the angst, guilt, and struggle. Obligation to everyone but myself! The move back to New Jersey with my last promotion was intended to be a good change for our marriage and the family. We had moved close to my parents and finally had help with the children. Unfortunately, this situation only manifested through more drinking, increasing anger, and bad behaviors on his part.

I went to see a divorce attorney. At that time, divorce in New Jersey was very cut and dry. You split the assets fifty-fifty, and a calculation was done in terms of income and alimony. As the breadwinner, I would have to pay him alimony. If he did not remarry, it would be for the rest of his life. It was a cold, stark reality shot to my gut. The attorney told me that everything I had worked for was in vain, and paying for two households would diminish the lifestyle of both families. She offered no counsel and no guidance, just doom and gloom. The children were angry with me and wanted their father home. They were too young to understand the seriousness of the situation. He promised he go to counseling. He seemed to make a genuine effort to get well. Considering the financial burden I was going to have to absorb, the children's pleas, and my ongoing guilt and stubbornness to think I could still fix the problem and save my family, I allowed him to return home with the promise that he would continue to seek help.

My career success continued. I was offered an executive position with another company making significantly more money. This allowed me to do even more to support my children financially and try to keep them safe. I hired an after-school nanny to drive the children to their activities, cook dinner and ensure their homework was done. Unfortunately, I could not rely on their father to do this. I would no longer place my children in danger. Although I had tried to give him another chance, the situation became even worse. He continued to drink. He became abusive emotionally, verbally, and sometimes physically. I never knew what I would come home to. Finally, when I came home one night, he was drunk and became very abusive. He scared me so much that I had to call the police. After that situation, I knew I had to move on, regardless of the financial consequences. I found a new, exceptional attorney that was supportive and provided excellent guidance. A yearlong battle ensued, but we finally settled and divorced in the summer of 2012.

A New Chapter

I became the sole supporter of my children emotionally, financially, affirmatively, informationally, and tangibly. I continued to struggle between career and family, but I had achieved peace of mind in terms of my children's safety and overall well-being. My growth in the financial services industry continued. I was offered a seat at the table as an executive leader, often the only woman in the room. As I participated in leadership panels and became involved with students at my alma mater, many people would reach out after hearing some of my story to ask for advice, guidance, or just ask, how did you do it? I realized that my experiences were not necessarily unique, and I could really help others. I wanted to help others, and I needed to help others. Whether it was a calling, a response to free myself of guilt, or maybe an understanding of how I can give back to help others in many of the same situations I had experienced, it was powerful and genuine. It really did not matter what compelled me, it was the right thing to do, and people needed help.

I thought a lot about the best way to help and leverage my experience to find financial freedom and peace of mind. I wanted to take my experience and expertise to the next level and really be able to make an impact on others' lives. COVID, the loss of a very dear friend, and a significant change in the company's work environment where I was employed were eventually the catalyst to take a deep dive into my current situation and purpose. I went back to school and obtained several certifications in life coaching, financial wellness, executive coaching and pursued my dream of self-employment. JM For Life was launched.

Reflections

I was one of the lucky ones. Because of my perseverance in both career and family, I was able to maintain my children's lifestyle. I kept them in their home, allowed them to pursue their interests and activities, maintained their social network, and tried to lead as healthy and happy a lifestyle as they could, even after the experience they had endured. The "golden nuggets" unearthed from my experience are as follows:

Values are extremely important, especially in a relationship. There needs to be upfront and open conversations about values, finances, and expectations. The concept of wanting to "save" someone, while noble, is overrated, often leads to difficult consequences, and rarely succeeds.

Both parties must contribute equally. It is not that each must earn the same income. However, each must contribute equally to the relationship. It must be a team effort with the sense of we are in this together. Finances are an essential factor. Statistics show that one of the main reasons why couples get divorced is because of financial challenges.

Self-awareness is critical. Becoming aware is the first step to creating meaningful change. Although I thought I was aware, I was really in denial. The pivotal moments where significant changes occurred were preceded by an "ah-hah" moment.

Of course, money has a monetary value. However, it also has a life value. We utilize the money to fund things we hold important based on our values. Therefore, financial freedom is very different and very personal to every individual. It means a lot of things to a lot of people. For me, it was the ability to leave my marriage. Once I became aware, I was able to channel my behaviors to reflect on what was most important to me and achieve my definition of financial freedom. A lot had to do with control.

I have been able to put my three children through college (the youngest is still attending), and I have tried to be a good role model in terms of love, values, morals, and family. I have been very fortunate to have a wonderful support system of family and friends. I was also able to pursue my passion of making a difference for others, starting a business, and finally finding a wonderful organization to work for that mirrors my values and my passions.

My purpose and motivation continues to be to help others — to be empowered, to be limitless, and to assist them with finding their own financial freedom.

Josephine Moran

Josephine Moran is the President and Chief Banking Officer for Ledyard National Bank in New Hampshire. In her role and in conjunction with the executive team, she creates strategies that provide financial solutions for the organization's clients and the local community. She also owns JM Fit for Life. Josephine is a Master Certified Life Coach and a Certified Financial Wellness Facilitator, executive coach, keynote speaker, and former licensed advisor.

With over twenty-five years of extensive experience in the financial services industry, the last ten years as a C-Suite executive, she has substantial expertise in community banking, investment services, residential and consumer lending, business banking, small business, customer experience, change leadership, digitization, modernization, marketing, strategy, leadership, and coaching. She has a proven track record of affecting change, motivating and influencing outcomes, and making a difference for individuals and organizations.

Moran is passionate about giving back. Her philanthropic activities support empowering women and DEI efforts, especially with her alma mater. She is a member of their Board of Governors, serves as Chairperson for the Pompea College of Business, and is the founder and chair of the Women's Leadership Council. She also serves on the Board of the YWCA of Union County and is an advisory council member of the Women's Business Collaborative.

Josephine was named Industry Era's "Top Ten Women Leaders in 2020." She has been featured in Entrepreneur Magazine, Independent Banker's Magazine, and in ThriveGlobal's "Meet the Female Leaders of Finance" series. She was named 2021 Top Women ROI Influencers by NJ Biz. Moran holds an Executive MBA from the University of New Haven and an M.S. in Finance and Financial Services. In addition, she holds Series 7 and 63 licenses.

Josephine is the proud mother of three and resides in Newtown, CT, with her significant other, Ron, and her daughter's black lab Zeus. She is an avid runner, a certified spin instructor, a huge music fan, and loves to read.

Josephine Moran
President and Chief Banking Officer
Ledyard Bank & Founder
JM Fit for Life
203-430-7326
Josephine.Moran@ledyardbank.com
JMFitForLife2@gmail.com
https://JMFitForLife1.com

Start Your Journey!

Receive your FREE Financial Wellness Survey and schedule your free consultation TODAY!

Awareness is the first step toward achieving financial freedom. This FREE survey will allow you to assess your thoughts, beliefs, behaviors, and results with money. It all begins with YOU!

- What is your relationship with money?

- How do your thoughts and beliefs impact your approach to money?

- How does your past experience impact your financial life?

https://JMFitForLife1.com/Offer

Amie Wade

We Get to Choose

W…T…F?!! Why is God doing this to me?

I thought He was supposed to be all-knowing and all-loving! Then, why is He allowing me to endure so much pain?

My life sucks, and I don't think I can keep doing this!

I'm so tired!

I wonder what life would be like for everyone, if I weren't here. Would they even really miss me? Did I really make that big of a difference anyway? They would probably be better off without me around.

I JUST CAN'T DO THIS ANYMORE!!

God, if you're real and you can hear me — why am I living this life? Why do I have to experience all this pain? Why do I have to live with this sadness… every… single… day? Crying all the time. I'm just so hurt and lost! There has got to be more to life than this! All the pain and anger that I'm carrying, I just want it to be over.

- *My biological father didn't love me enough to hang around, leaving my mom shortly after he found out she was pregnant.*

- *My mom chose the two emotionally and mentally abusive men as her husbands to live in our home — yeah, I'm angry at them **and** her for this!!*

- *Then, if that wasn't enough, God, you tossed in the molestation too!*

Really??!! What did I do to deserve all this? Why would I be given this *life to have to go through, and then the end result is to die, at whatever age that may be? There definitely **must** be more to life than this!!*

This is the conversation I had nearly every day from the age of fourteen (the age I was when the molestation occurred) into my mid-thirties. If you're not aware, there is a lot of shame associated with being molested, which diminishes all hope. I was constantly exhausted from not only the shame, but also the intense amount of anger; the guilt; the criticisms and judgments from myself; the feeling that I don't deserve this life, nor do I belong here; and the thought — yes, daily — of ending my life. I didn't know the purpose of life, and frankly, after the molestation experience, I didn't really care.

I didn't know what it was at the time, but there was something in me that said, "Keep showing up — just keep going" — it was like a mantra, but it wasn't me saying it. This "something" was an inner strength that I didn't know how to explain. Obviously, I listened to it — I'm still here!

In the meantime, I didn't know what to do with all the painful emotions that were bottled up inside me. If you had an upbringing like mine, you would have been told things like, "Stop crying, or I'll give you something to cry about!" "Suck it up. You're fine!" "Don't be a cry baby!" "Go to your room if you're going to cry!"

There weren't any instructions from the adults around me on how to deal with these painful emotions in a healthy manner. So, the practice was to just suppress it and keep going!

Eventually, I found my solution — alcohol. Oh, yes, we're talking the hard stuff because I wasn't much of a beer drinker at the time. However, I later acquired a taste for that too. It all gave me a considerable amount of emotional relief. I could finally relax and have a good time! When I was intoxicated, I laughed and danced — **I felt good!** Remember the 1980's TV sitcom *"Cheers"* when Norm would enter the bar, everyone knew him, and they would all say in unison "NORM!"? I pretty much reached that status — it was more like, "Amie's here!" and, well, it may not have been everyone saying it, but there were a lot of people who did. The joy, the connection, the acceptance, the love — now *this* is what I'm talking about — **I can do this!**

My drunken nights, vomiting to the porcelain God, and hangover mornings continued for several years. I knew, however, that alcohol wasn't the answer for the long term. I needed to figure out an alternative because my body would not be able to sustain itself with the amount of tequila and beer I was consuming. Frankly, it was getting more difficult to recover. Ugh!! I also had a son that needed my love and attention. How could I truly love him, if I don't even know how to love myself? How can I be a good mom and teach him to navigate life, if I don't even know how? I still questioned God every day and needed to know if this was what life was all about until the day we die. I had to find an alternative solution!

You see, what I recognized was that I was blaming God, my mom, my biological father, my two stepdads, the molester — and let's include all the boyfriends and anyone else that made my life seem like hell — for how I was showing up in my life — unloved, not accepted, angry and depressed with suicidal thoughts. I was pointing the finger at everyone else because that's what I knew how to do. They needed to apologize or change, in order for my life to be better. What I didn't know was that by blaming them for my way of being, *I was giving them the power over me.* I decided that I wanted to take back my power. I could do this by learning about and growing within myself.

I'm going to tell you straight up, I was scared to release the life of "Norm" because it was comfortable and fun. I couldn't imagine being able to relax and have as much fun without alcohol. What if my "friends" didn't like me anymore because I chose not to drink?

I will tell you from the point of view from where I am right now — I'M ENJOYING MY LIFE SO MUCH MORE! Was it an easy transformation? Hell no!!! It was tough getting to know me — who *I* am and what *I* like (notice the emphasis on "I"). You see, some of the behaviors I took on from a child were being a "people pleaser," a "fixer," and a "control freak," which meant

I was living most of my life *for* others — doing what **they** liked and wanted to do and then being the bitchy control freak because, well, I was still out of control. I wanted the love and acceptance but knew deep down — again, the "inner knowing" — that living my life *for them* wasn't fulfilling to me.

Remember that inner strength and voice that said, "Keep showing up — just keep going?" Well, what I believe to be true, is that it was my *spirit* talking to me. By blaming others, I allowed "them" to break me. However, my spirit was much more powerful. It was up to me to listen to it! Spirit is love, and I have come to understand and accept that I am a spirit in a body living a human life. Therefore, *I am already love and loved*! When I chose to have a deeper connection with my spirit, it fueled my desire to have the emotional resilience to keep showing up for my life. I was then guided in the direction of shifting my mindset from "WTF?!!" (WHAT THE FUCK?!!) to "Wtf?" (What's this **for**?), by asking powerful questions, such as:

- "Why is this happening *for* me?"

- "What am I *learning* about myself through this experience?"

- "What *knowledge or wisdom* did I gain because of that situation?"

These types of questions allow me to have a different perspective about life challenges, contribute to how I show up in my life, and shift to experiencing joy more often. Questions like these also took me from being a victim of my life to claiming my power, being more in control of my life, and allowing me to step into my greatness.

I recognized that I needed to get past my self-defeating thoughts. The thoughts were telling me I was worthless, unlovable, and unaccepted. The underlying story of it all was... *I'm not good enough!* Thoughts like these kept me in the tailspin of depression, and if I believed the stories that I was telling myself, then, of course, they were true.

When you are experiencing lower vibrational emotions like shame, guilt, anger, resentment, grief, or despair, it causes a lot of stress in the body. It is unbeknownst to you because you've been in that state of being for so long. Stress is the #1 cause of most diseases. Lower vibrational emotions (l.v.e.) need some *love* to transform to higher vibrational emotions like hopefulness, optimism, enthusiasm, exhilaration, and joy. One thing you can do right away, is to change your self-talk and the stories you've been telling yourself.

You get to write the script! From my perspective, you're a badass for having this Earth life because it takes a lot of courage, strength, and endurance. Therefore, tell yourself empowering stories of survival, strength, courage, and determination and acknowledge the wisdom you have gained. Wisdom is powerful! You had an experience that didn't turn out so good, *so what!* You figure out what worked and what didn't work (be sure to also account for your own behaviors and actions here). You implement what you learned, and then you have the wisdom to help you as you continue to navigate your life.

Affirmations are a great tool to help shift your perspective about life. I personally didn't like the idea of affirmations because I didn't believe what I was telling myself. In this case, "fake it till you make it" didn't work, so I found a way to make them more believable. Insert the word "choose" or "allow" — for example, instead of saying "I am amazing!" say "I choose to see how amazing I am!" or "I am worthy of love" to "I allow love to flow to me." From this perspective, I'm also giving myself a choice — do it or not — and I would rather do something that feels good to me.

Redirect your focus from the negative stories you are telling yourself to right here, right now. Presence — this is all we have. You can't change the past — it's already done — and the future isn't guaranteed. We only have **this** moment and what you do with it is up to you. You can either feel good — or at least feel better — or continue the path of what doesn't feel good.

My ability to experience joy more often comes from the basis of me loving myself more. It's up to me to fill my cup up. It's nobody's job to love me. It's my job. It's nobody's job to make me happy. It's my job. My life, my responsibility! I could choose to stay a victim to my circumstances and expect someone else to make it all better, or I could choose to rise out of the depression. It really was always my choice. Just like being healthier is my choice, no one can make me change my eating habits or exercise. To be financially secure is my choice; no one can make me invest my money wisely. I had to stop expecting someone to come to save me from all the emotional pain and take action in improving the way I was feeling.

I have a spirit in my body that came to this planet for a reason, for growth and expansion, to feel emotions, to have experiences, and also to have fun. From my victim mindset, I thought, "What-the-fuck-was-my-spirit-thinking?" I was thinking this way because I hadn't yet looked outside of the walls to see all the ways that I could make a shift in my life to experience joy. I had to open my eyes, look around and be open to all the amazing things on this planet we get to enjoy. I'm ecstatic to know that I get to choose to be limitless!

Amie Wade

Amie Wade is a Certified Life Coach; Certified Mindy, Body, Spirit Practitioner; Reiki Master/Teacher; Certified Angel Card Reader; Certified 200-hour yoga teacher; and author. She has a background of over 20 years of office management and administration work. She was an owner/operator and partner of a convenience store/gas station/deli for seven years, until the 2008 economic downturn. She has been a guest on the Radio Central Speak Out 2.0 KNTR FM located in Laughlin, Nevada, Off The Cuff Podcast with Sunny Dawn Johnston, and guest speaker at Soroptimist International of Kingman.

Hanging onto her childhood stories of abandonment, mental and emotional abuse and then molestation, which contributed to having suicidal thoughts almost daily, kept her in the space of hopelessness and despair. As an adult, she chose to use alcohol to cope with her unhealthy emotions and a way to be able to relax and have fun. With the information she gained from taking the certification courses, reading lots of books, and listening to a multitude of spiritual teachers and influencers, she learned to change her perspective about her life experiences and released her addiction.

While working full-time in the corporate world, Amie dabbled in coaching for 15 years with her Reiki clients and the classes, workshops, and retreats that she facilitated. She decided that her desire and lifelong mission is to help guide others in feeling empowered as they navigate their emotional healing journey with the intention of being confident in living a spiritual-based life with a powerful sense of self-love and, therefore, established her business as Amie Wade — Emotional Resiliency Coach, LLC.

She currently resides in Arizona with Aaron, her hubby of 23 years. She has one son, Matthew, and a granddog, Amerah (means princess — and she is!).

Amie Wade
Emotional Resiliency Coach, LLC
Kingman, AZ
928-487-0964
Support@AmieWade.com
https://AmieWade.com
Linktr.ee/AmieWade

Techniques for Less Stress

Most stress is created from the fear-based mind chatter we have based on past experiences or about future events. Receive a workbook and video series with techniques to help you embrace and enjoy the present moment more often.

https://AmieWade.com/FreeGift

Kelley Tenny

EmPOWERing Through Education

I can still remember my first A.

It was in the form of a happy face sticker. I was only in preschool when I earned it, but that doesn't change the memory. My teacher smiled at me as she handed my work back to me. I stared down at that bright yellow, smiley face sticker. Next to it was "Good job!" in my teacher's beautiful, neat handwriting.

At pick-up, I could barely contain my excitement. My mom got me into the car, and I excitedly pulled out my folder. "Look, mom!" I shouted from the back seat, as I held my paper up.

"Good girl!" she replied. "Let's get more of those, ok?"

I nodded with excitement, confident that I could do it. I got to put my paper on the refrigerator at home. When my dad walked in from work, I earned a "Good" and a pat on the head from him. I went to bed beaming.

It was a proud day, and more importantly, a monumental day that set the tone for my academic journey. My future was limitless.

Education and the importance of academics differs from family to family. In some, it is the one priority that families will sacrifice for. However, in others, it's seen as a luxury that only comes second to finding good work and providing for your family. Can you guess what my family's views were about education?

An "A" was like winning the Pulitzer Prize in my house. And a bad grade was, well...

My freshman year of high school, in my U.S. History class, during a typical period of passing back tests, my teacher crossed in front of my desk and laid down my test facedown. FACEDOWN! I knew what that meant. It had never happened to me before, but I KNEW what that meant. The grade on the other side of that paper was not an A. And more than likely, not a B or a C.

I was mortified. The showing up naked to school, kind of mortified. I flipped the paper over to see a red "D+" staring me right in the face. I quickly put my paper away before anyone could see it.

You can imagine the shock and outright disappointment that I was greeted with, once my parents found out about my grade. It was made clear that grades like that were unacceptable. I was scolded for not studying hard enough, being "stupid," and reminded that people who get grades like that have no future.

While this may not seem like a harsh punishment compared to what it could have been, the disappointment and retraction of affection and emotion from my parents was worse than any period of being grounded could have done. I had been put into solitary emotional confinement and sent to my cell with a scarlet letter on my chest. My letter was a big "F" for failure.

I felt stupid, ashamed, and unlovable.

Of course, my school journey went on. I continued to be highly successful, graduating with honors in both high school and college, with little help from parents or other adults. However, I had learned something. I learned to become the student chameleon, shifting and shaping to the variety of teachers and teaching styles that each class I took presented me.

I did EVERYTHING I could to get A's and was fortunate to have developed the skills needed to do so.

Shortly before I graduated from college with a Bachelor of Science in both Community Health and School Health, my academic advisor called me in to see what plans I had after graduation. She shared with me that there was a shortage of teachers in our state and encouraged me to consider going into teaching Health.

Having a solid job right out of college appealed to me, as did the schedule of a teacher (you see, the life-long learner in me had plans to move on and get my masters). Into the classroom, I went.

I landed at a middle school in North Long Beach, CA. The school was in a low-income neighborhood that was riddled with gang activity. My students came from all different demographics and backgrounds.

It wasn't long until I started to realize that I wasn't reaching all of my students. Many of them "weren't getting it." Unlike myself as a child, many of them weren't equipped with my student chameleon skills — the skills to figure out how to learn effectively from the methods I was using to teach. It wasn't just happening in my classroom. These students were academically suffering across the board.

I wondered how many of these students were feeling "stupid" and ashamed, much like I had, every time they received a poor letter grade. What was this doing to their confidence and self-esteem?

How could I teach in ways that would meet the learning needs of all my students?

That single question led me to pursue my Master of Education in Curriculum and Instruction. I studied how educational programs should be created and implemented, so that all students could learn and feel academic success. I soaked up what I was learning and began to let it guide the way I taught with limitless possibilities.

If you've ever taken a class or a course where you struggled to keep up or grasp the concepts, you have been in the same place as these students. Feelings of confusion, inadequacy, shame, and often defeat were common in the school where I taught. My goal was to make sure that stopped when they entered my door. I strived to do just that, for every single one of my students, for the next 15 years.

As my time in the classroom went on and I began to start my own family, I started to look for more flexible options outside of the classroom. However, it was never far from education. My journey led me into the entrepreneurial world. It was full of genius, information, and opportunities.

They say you can take the teacher out of the classroom, but you will never take the classroom out of the teacher. That could not have been truer for me. I attended webinars, read blogs, and signed up for every online course possible to learn how to make my business successful. The options to learn were limitless in this new educational arena.

I spent hundreds, even thousands of dollars on courses to learn all the strategies that I needed to launch my business, from strategies to skills and even courses on mindset. Strangely, I found many of these courses challenging in more ways than one.

I had a hard time keeping up with some of the courses, especially those that were self-led. I found them confusing and got behind the suggested schedule. I often felt isolated. I didn't have classmates that I could collaborate with and lean on for support.

I was blasted back in time to the same humiliation that I felt during my freshman year in high school.

There was so much expertise and knowledge at my fingertips, yet so much of it was just beyond my reach… and not just mine.

Entrepreneurs all around me were investing thousands in courses that they could not finish or didn't effectively learn from. Feelings of shame and stupidity arose for spending so much money with little to nothing to show for it. Imposter syndrome and self-doubt crept in. I became the struggling student in the classroom.

Suddenly, everything I had learned about teaching and delivering education was right back in front of me. The challenges that I witnessed with formal education also existed in continuing education. I was among leaders who wanted to share their skills and expertise with others. I was among coaches, consultants, and entrepreneurs who desired to learn things that formal education had not taught them.

Yet, it was all slightly out of reach. Experts were charging hundreds, sometimes thousands of dollars for their courses. However, they were impossible to learn from. Some were a series of downloads, and others were just a bunch of audio or video files. Other courses required participants to show up on video calls, to be talked at for an hour. If participants were lucky, a weekly Q and A was included, which fueled comparison and more confusion.

It lit a fire in me. These experts were making thousands of dollars and taking people's money. They were people who wanted to learn a skill or concept, so that they could be more successful. The courses were pieced together and often topped off with glitz and glamour to mask the fact that it was simply a pretty packaged pile of information. In fact, it was the piles of information that made it almost impossible for someone to learn effectively. I knew the quantity of content didn't equal quality education.

A light bulb went on.

This was why so many others around me were taking course after course and spending endless amounts of money in an attempt to learn to build their businesses. This was why people bought courses and never finished them. This is why online education was frowned upon by so many.

It wasn't the fault of the experts. They had a desire to help others and desperately wanted to teach what they knew. They spent hours wondering why their clients were dissatisfied and not taking action on what the course taught them. The time spent dealing with refunds and extra support took time away from them building their business.

How could they know how to create a sound educational course that truly shared their knowledge and yielded amazing results for their clients?

However, I knew.

I could see clearly with my educational training, the training and experience from years ago when I was in the middle school classroom. The educational framework I knew so well could be applied to this new level of education. There were small but crucial pieces that were missing from these courses. They could easily be put into place and drastically increase the success rate of the participants.

This was when Teach Your Brilliance was born. It is a course development company that would allow my educational background, love for learning, and the wide world of entrepreneurship to support experts of all areas in creating online courses based on educational research and framework. They are courses that changed the businesses and lives of the participants.

This was my chance to rehabilitate education as we knew it, by placing quality courses in the hands of almost anyone. It involved limitlessly transforming lives through the power of education.

What if we as a society collectively pooled our knowledge and expertise with others, so that they were empowered to pay it forward and make a difference in the world today?

What if my children had limitless options for quality education outside of college and universities, both of which are honorable establishments, yet not without their own challenges and issues that students face today?

Through my own journey as a learner and later as an educator, I have learned and witnessed the limitless power that education holds. I have formed a belief, which I am committed to making a reality, that continuing education can be reformed when we mix educationally structured courses with the insight and mastery of the experts among us.

They should be experts who are ready to share the unique knowledge and secrets that got them to where they are today, ready to knock down the dominoes and shape trails to success for others.

Are you ready to teach your brilliance and transform the lives of others? Are you ready to open up a new world of accessible education?

Could this be you? Ask yourself:

Do I Have Something to Teach?

Do you know a lot about something that others also want to learn more about? You are then one step toward being ready to create an online course. First, find out if the topic or subject you know a lot about is in demand. Ask yourself, what is it that you know that many others also want to know? Then, create your online course on this topic or subject matter.

Am I an Expert in One Area?

If yes, then create and sell courses related to everything you're best at. Your expertise is your greatest gift to others. When you create an online course, be sure to create one that relates to what you know best and what you are most passionate about.

Am I Ready to Generate a Broader Impact by Sharing My Knowledge with Other People Around the World by Creating My Own Online Course(s)?

When we create courses on subjects that we're experts in, there is nothing more fulfilling than seeing the positive impact it has had on other people's lives. Creating an online course generates a greater impact on your community because you are able to place all of your expertise in one place. This makes it more accessible to your audience.

My invitation is for you to join me. Join me in this transformational movement, where together, we can share our wealth of knowledge and empower others through accessible, quality education and generate a greater impact on our society.

"When experts of all areas choose to share their brilliance by educating others, it is then that we can make the world a better place."

—Kelley Tenny

Kelley Tenny

Kelley Tenny, a "life-long learner," has a passion for learning that can be traced back to her early childhood education. Born and raised in a household of high expectations, she strived to excel in school and could always be found with her nose in a book.

Her educational journey brought her to Long Beach for college, where her passion for health and wellness led Kelley to pursue a degree in health education. Her desire to go into public health was detoured when her college mentor told her that she would make a great health teacher. During a time when California was suffering a teacher shortage, Kelley's love for learning, education, and desire to serve others took over, and she stepped foot inside her first classroom in inner-city Long Beach.

And this is where her "detour" as a teacher turned into a passion for empowering others through learning.

Years of teaching experience, in middle school and later on at the university level, unveiled that not all people found learning easy. Barriers like teaching methods, distracting environments, poorly written curriculum, and accessibility issues made it difficult for students to find success in the educational setting.

What if education could not only be created to meet the needs of the learners but be placed at their fingertips as well, removing barriers like transportation and cost, to name a few?

It was then that Teach Your Brilliance was born. Kelley founded a company that supports others in teaching their brilliance by creating online courses that are embedded in entrepreneurial pedagogy and delivered in a variety of ways to meet all the needs of possible students.

Kelley saw that this could be the way to shift education as we know it by removing so many of the barriers that are found in traditional education. And what better way to empower than to inspire other educators, authors, coaches, and consultants to share their brilliance with others?

Now a married mom of two, she resides in Long Beach and continues to not only teach college but also develop curriculum and create online courses for entrepreneurs that are ready to be a part of this educational movement.

Kelley Tenny
Teach Your Brilliance
Long Beach, CA
714-235-2112
TeachYourBrilliance@gmail.com
TeachYourBrilliance.com

Are You Ready to Teach Your Brilliance?

You may be called to share your wealth of knowledge with the world but don't know where to start. Or perhaps you wonder if you have the expertise needed to teach others! This free ebook will reveal the three things that you need to create an online course that effectively educates others. You may be surprised that you already have them! So get ready to empower others with your wisdom, generate life-long clients, and create an infinite revenue stream. It's time to teach your brilliance.

KelleyTenny.ac-page.com/3-Thing-You-Need-to-Create-Your-Online-Course

Christy Lister

The Invisible Badge

Monday, June 17th, 2019, started out typically. My phone started ringing early. I looked at it and didn't recognize the number, so I let it go to voicemail. A few minutes passed, and I got a text; "Christy, this is the Chief of Police. Are you home?" My first reaction was gut-wrenching. If you could feel someone ripping out every morsel of your being, that was it. However, I had to keep myself together. OK, OK, OK, I got this. I texted back, "Do not come to my front door. I will meet you by my garage. Do not come anywhere near my front door. I cannot let the kids see you yet." I was not ready to have them know what was coming next.

My mind was processing, as I walked outside to hear the words, "Christy… We are sorry to inform you that Ken has died." I tried to gather myself, as The Chief of Police, a liaison for the department, two detectives, and a chaplain all stood in front of me. I looked at them, and told myself, "Don't let them see the fear, sadness, and loss of words as they talk." Here it goes, the feeling of heartbreak pouring through my body, like lava overflowing through my skin. I asked, "How did this happen?" *Ken died by suicide.* My mind said, let those words sink in. What did I miss? Typically, when the Chief comes to the door it's because of a line of duty incident, but deep down I knew this would not be the case. Why did I miss this over a 25-year period? Were the signs always there? Did I see them and choose not to address them? After all, we were divorced. How can this be happening? How did I fail him and the kids? A law enforcement family prepares mentally for this call and always hopes it never happens. But here we are, now what? I took a second to internalize the words I had just heard. Nothing prepares you for this moment. I had no idea how I would react next. I just knew that I had to be there for the kids, and I had to be strong for them.

I took a moment, counting the rocks that had formed from the broken hot black asphalt in the driveway. I slowly brought my head up and said, "How do I tell the kids?" The Chief said, "That's why we are here for you." I did everything I could to prevent tears in my eyes because I must go inside, look our beautiful kids in the eyes, and tell them their dad isn't coming home. I must take this moment and make sure I am present for the kids. I asked everyone to wait outside until I could get the kids up and on the couch. *It was so surreal.* My oldest was awake watching TV. He was never up early, and he had no idea I had walked outside. The dogs were quiet. Even though they saw the group of people walking to the driveway, they are never quiet. I had to go and wake up the other two kids. I had to ask them to go sit on the couch and wait there for me. I saw the image of the look in their eyes, as they were trying to understand why they must sit there together is forever playing in my head. I went out and got the group of policemen and the chaplain. We quietly start walking. The liaison looked at me and said, "Christy, we tried to help Ken." Those words hit me like a ton of bricks. What does this mean? I internally marked these words to address later. The task of saying, "Your dad isn't coming home again," had to come out of my mouth. I had to be there for the kids to help with questions, even though I had no answers. It felt like an out-of-body experience. I was standing there talking, but I could see us all standing there. I saw the disbelief and shock on the kids' faces as the words rolled off my tongue. The Chief did the best he could to stand strong. He was still in as much disbelief as we were. The department lost a family member that day, too.

The day Ken died, everything fell on my oldest, since he was the next of kin. Ken didn't have a will or trust, so all the decisions had to be made. There is no way a 19-year-old should ever have to make decisions on planning the wake or all of his financials. My oldest was a sophomore in college. It was supposed to be the fun years in life. Yet, dealing with the loss of his dad weighed heavily on his shoulders. We decided that I would help guide the decisions of everything, all while keeping the three kids informed of everything going on. The police department helped make sure Ken was honored in the best way they could. Even though Ken's wishes were to have a full police funeral if he were to die, this couldn't happen. Ken's struggles were brought on by the job. However, they are not considered line of duty struggles. They are considered personal struggles. You see, when an officer dies by suicide, it is not considered a line-of-duty death. Therefore, his death was not considered a line-of-duty death. Ken gave 25 years of his life serving and protecting the community. Everything he saw and dealt with is more than most people will ever see in a lifetime. The police department did an amazing job trying to help guide us through this issue and support us the best they could. At the funeral, Ken had the honor guard standing next to him, and the chief stood with us the entire time. Ken's many Chief Awards and SWAT Awards were displayed, including the one he was given for saving someone else from dying by suicide. Let that sink in a moment. Ken saved someone from taking their own life, only to turn around and have that moment of feeling so defeated and broken that he ended up taking his own life.

It took me 25 years of service as a family member to realize I was putting on a badge every day. My badge was invisible. It didn't seem to weigh me down. It protected me from the dents of the world, the crossfire of the job. Or did it? Honestly, the weight of an invisible badge is heavy. The misunderstood position of how family members of officers who are considered civilians play a vital role in the Police family is greatly misguided and undervalued. I completely understand the need to protect your spouse, kids, parents, and siblings from what you see on the job every day. It's hard to remove your emotions to get the job done, but it's even harder to continue to engage your emotions for your family when processing the last call you were on before coming home to your life. It is equally important to realize that your family is serving right next to you. The difference is, we don't know why emotions become separated. We internalize it as something we have done or caused undue stress as you come home and remain disengaged. We are processing what is happening without knowing what or why it's happening. We are taking the hits to our invisible badge daily. We feel that strike against our badge and the pain that comes with it when it hits you so hard, you feel it pierce your soul. The truth is, we don't know how to process what is happening either, so we often sit in silence, do our part to try and be there for you, for the job, and pretend like we understand.

IT'S OK TO NOT BE OK

Family doesn't need to take off that invisible badge. We just need to learn to process what we don't understand because we are not being told. The first thing to remember: **IT'S OK TO NOT BE OK**. Please repeat that to yourself. **IT'S OK TO NOT BE OK**. It's also OK for your Law Enforcement Officer to not be OK. Straighten your badge, don't be afraid to start talking, and let them know you are seeing changes in them. Let them know if you are struggling to process what you are feeling. We don't know what we don't know. Once you realize that **IT'S OK TO NOT BE OK**, then you can start to feel the pain of the unknown. Feeling pain isn't always going to hurt if you can find a healthy way to remove it from the core of your soul. There are many ways to help process, such as counseling, journaling, or talking to a friend.

Your Law Enforcement Officer may struggle when you tell them that you are struggling. That is OK! They have most likely been thinking all along they have been protecting you from the job. They may be in disbelief that you are struggling from the job, which is partly due to their own disbelief that they are struggling. For years, they thought they were protecting you from the crossfire and thought they were dealing with it by talking to the guy's off shift about a call. However, what is happening is they aren't processing. They are deflecting. They then get in the car to go home and find other ways to deflect what they view as a weakness, the feelings that have been buried deep inside for so many years. You may notice little changes that trigger a red flag, but you have spent so many years deflecting yourself. Small changes occur over time, so they become easily undetected. The small things add up slowly. They can become emotionally detached from the family, spends extra money they don't have, or stays out longer than usual after a shift. They could also use any other unhealthy coping skills that they have chosen to get that quick fix of, "See, I dealt with it, I am fine." You need to know that this is happening. *It's OK not to recognize it at first. I just want you to recognize it before it's too late.*

As a first responder family member, a normal reaction is to not talk about the struggles in the home life. I want you to stop right there. We can't change anything if we don't talk about change. There are many tools that you can add to your toolbox to help yourself, your officers, and your children — starting with caring for yourself first. You can't care for anyone else, if you don't fill your cup with the correct fuel. First Responders and their families are a special breed of people, and many people, including some of our own families, don't understand.

YOU ARE NOT ALONE

There are resources for you and your family that can help you find the tools you need to process the job and bring your family to a safe and healthy place in life. Life will always throw unexpected things at us, but we can make a difference in each other's life by having conversations about mental health being normal. If you are looking for resources, you can check out Blue H.E.L.P and click on resources. It will provide you with family support, training, and by clicking on the 1sthelp tab, you can find someone in your area who specializes in first responders and their families. You are not alone!

FIRST H.E.L.P. Beyond the 1st Response Podcast

A podcast that brings first responders, families, and mindset together for serious and humorous conversations on mental health.

https://1stHelp.org/podcast

Christy Lister

Christy Lister is the former wife of a law enforcement officer who died by suicide. She is the mother of three beautiful and resilient children who tragically lost their father on June 17th, 2019. Christy was introduced to Blue H.E.L.P., a national not-for-profit that helps Honor, Educate, Lead, and Protect law enforcement and their families, helping to break the mental health stigma in Law Enforcement. Christy has been volunteering with Blue Help since September of 2019. She speaks with Police Departments and families on breaking the stigma of mental health, the signs, and policies changes that can be made. It's OK Not To Be OK!

Christy Lister
Blue H.E.L.P.
Plainfield, IL
815-955-9970
Christy@BlueHelp.org
www.1stHelp.org

First H.E.L.P.

First Help is a searchable database dedicated to finding emotional, financial, and spiritual assistance for first responders. In addition to assisting first responders in finding crisis-specific help, it will collect data on suicide and traumatic-stress events. This information will be used to save lives and improve the quality of life for first responders. This tool will always be free to first responders, and there is no charge to register your organization to be listed in the database.

https://BlueHelp.org/resources/1sthelp

Elaine Joyce Gibson

Are You Waiting for a Crisis?

The problem: 39.5 percent of men and women will be diagnosed with cancer. 23.5 million Americans suffer from an autoimmune disease, and 39.6 percent of adults have obesity.

Elaine Gibson here. I was just like you, and this is what happened to me.

I remember the day I fell to my knees on my beautiful needlepoint rug. I can still taste the salt as the tears ran down my face.

That was the day that my medical team told me that I had stage four non-Hodgkin's lymphoma (NHL). They did not believe that I would live to see my grandchildren grow up. Seriously. How does anybody say that to a Jewish grandmother from New York City? I guess they hadn't met the mama bear species before.

I looked up and said, "OK, God, I know I'm not going to die. Just tell me what you want me to learn."

The journey began, as I searched to figure out what the real foundation of health is at the cellular level. What do the healthiest people do?

I knew that the traditional protocol was not for me as my first line of offense. Putting toxins in my body when I actually felt that this was exactly what got me here was not my preference. There had to be a path I could trust.

I'm an athlete, so I went into training.

This is important for you to know.

You catch the flu, but you don't catch cancer or any other chronic diseases. It is an inside job. You are the one who creates it through your actions, choices, and decisions. Even though you may believe you are living a healthy lifestyle, you don't get symptoms until it's often too late. You do it to yourself, and you are the only ones who can undo it.

You do not have control over so much, but you have 100 percent control over what goes into your body. This is great, great news.

You do not have to wait for a crisis.

There Is Magic in the Whispers

Inspired by Oprah and her concept about how our body is always whispering to us, I became more aware of what was going on.

Your body is always talking to you, but you are so busy living in the fast lane that you don't stop to listen. You are designed to be healthy and to function beautifully.

The answers for relieving symptoms that you are experiencing, whether extra pounds, exhaustion, inflammation, or chronic ailments, are all there. The answers to creating your extraordinary health are birthed in the whispers that your body gives you, but you are not listening because you are too busy.

Here are several examples of early whispers:

- Headache
- Heartburn
- Back pain
- Sleeplessness
- Exhaustion
- Weight gain
- Lack of focus
- Constipation
- Dizziness

- Depression

These symptoms become so familiar that you begin to believe they are a natural part of aging. Not true.

No, no, no, no, no. That's not how you are supposed to be. You deserve to experience optimal health, vitality, and joy every day.

Somehow, we have become a society that treats the symptoms, not the underlying causes.

You deserve better. You've heard me say it before, and you will hear me say it again.

You Deserve Better.

When your body starts to whisper, it's in response to the symptoms that are showing up. It is how the universe gets your attention. Not only is the answer in the whispers, but they reflect your cumulative patterns and habits in your lifestyle.

Start to look back at what you were doing thirty days, sixty days, ninety days prior. You will uncover the choices that led to the warning signs.

You are the result of all the decisions that you have made.

As you begin to understand and embrace the fact you have control over your health and well-being, you can begin to answer the whispers.

There is magic in the whispers.

I come in contact with many amazing, beautifully busy women who are taking care of everybody else and somehow forget to take care of themselves.

The greatest act of being unselfish is taking the time for yourself. The people you love are counting on this.

Self-care is not selfish.

Are You Sick and Tired of the Weight?

Maybe it's the extra pounds that have you frustrated because you can't zip your favorite jeans or just the weight of everyday life, everyday experiences, and everyday overwhelm that is all around us.

As you continue this life's journey, your body is filled with calories, and your cells are craving nutrients. Your cells are starving. When this happens, your body is in crisis mode; nothing works well.

It is important that you understand that those unwanted pounds and the extra weight of life are linked to other things that are showing up. Carrying around extra pounds can play havoc on you.

You are designed to thrive in Nature. I like to think of the journey as the stepping-stones through God's garden. It keeps me grounded, and it keeps me making choices that come from Nature.

You have been taught that everybody puts on weight with age. It's not true. Extra weight is dangerous. It carries toxins that compromise your health.

Fad diets take you down temporary roads that never last. You need and deserve a sustainable lifestyle straight from God's garden.

When I was fighting for my life, I turned to nature for solutions. I lost twenty-eight pounds and four dress sizes. I created a simple, intentional, sustainable lifestyle that keeps me looking and feeling better than ever before.

It is not about dieting. It is about eating for radiance. It's about saying yes to yourself, instead of no.

You are exhausted from attempting to make good healthy choices amidst the noise. Decision fatigue sets in, and you defer to your status quo because making new choices requires a clear mind and energy.

The status quo is stealing your dreams.

Women share that they just cannot learn or do one more thing. Actually, eating for radiance is the easiest enhancement you can make. You are eating anyway. You merely swap out choices.

This is not like going to the gym! Please tell me I am not the only one with a fitness membership that is not being used.

The key is to shed your unwanted pounds, increase your energy, create disease-free, optimal health naturally and realistically, without feeling deprived, disrupting your busy life — or even giving up chocolate.

The Fountain of Youth

I didn't know, what I didn't know!

Here is what I learned: the food we eat, the water we drink, and even the air we breathe can throw off our body's natural balance, interfere with our health, and accelerate the aging process.

It is all about the immune system!

To function properly, every cell in your body needs an alkaline, oxygen-rich environment. *This could be considered the fountain of youth.*

Maya Angelou has taught us: "When you know better, you do better."

The concept of alkalinity never came up, until I entered my health journey in 2008. I *thought* I was leading a healthy lifestyle.

Here are three simple, actionable ideas you can begin to use right away.

Add these seven most alkaline foods: spinach, broccoli, celery, cucumbers, kale, bell peppers, and avocado to your food plan.

Begin your day with hot water and lemon. This will hydrate you and increase your focus, energy, and elimination.

Reduce sugar, dairy, and wheat.

Looking back, there are two key steps I took immediately that ultimately saved my life:

1. I never, for one second, believed that I was going to die. I trusted that God had a plan for me, even if that plan would not be revealed for some time. I knew I would live to see this plan out.

2. I took complete control over educating myself about the foundation

of health and a strong immune system.

You Deserve Better!

Imagine having an abundance of real energy throughout the day and loving the way you look and feel.

Imagine living a life where disease simply cannot find a home.

Your body, mind, and soul work together to keep you happy, healthy, and living an extraordinary life! You deserve to dance vibrantly and youthfully, in your own unique style.

This is my dream for you.

Elaine Joyce Gibson

Elaine Gibson is an extraordinary woman. She was cited as one of the world's top ten natural cancer survivors by Extreme Health Radio. Having beaten Stage IV cancer without traditional protocols, Elaine shares her hard-won lessons for living a clean, healthy, and natural lifestyle. Once she began making healthy changes, she lost twenty-eight pounds and dropped four to five clothing sizes. Elaine, the founder of Renewed Living, is a published author, sought-after motivational speaker, workshop facilitator, and private coach.

For the last several years, Elaine Gibson has trained and coached high-achieving women in a new way of approaching their lifestyles — by harnessing the power of positive intention to create an extraordinary life to regain their zest and step into their own version of extraordinary. She works from the principle that it is possible through natural clean living to counteract the stressful and health-damaging effects that modern living has on the body, mind, and relationships. The women she works with love to feel good about themselves and learn how to get there with the least amount of hassle and confusion.

Elaine has been featured in VA Woman Magazine, the award-winning film Cancer: The Integrative Perspective, The Global Cancer Symposium, Take Back Your Health Conferences in Washington, DC, and California, Inspiring Women, Unscripted Power, Cure 2 Cancer Conference, Annie Appleseed Cancer Conference, and the Quest for the Cures documentary series. She is a contributing author to the newly released books Don't Waste My Cancer and Midlife Transformations.

Her proudest accomplishment is being a green juice-loving grandmother.

Elaine Joyce Gibson
Renewed Living
114 Song Sparrow Drive
Lake Frederick, VA 22630
703-622-6885
Elaine@RenewedLivingInc.com
www.RenewedLivingInc.com

14 Days to an Extraordinary New You!

Elaine's signature diet is unique. As a disease prevention expert and health coach, she understands bio-individuality. This program is designed to help YOU learn what foods fuel YOUR unique body, as well as the exercise routines, health, and de-stressing strategies that work for YOUR unique life and schedule.

- You CAN live a life free from confusion about what to eat, where you feel completely in control of your body and mind.

- Lose weight quickly and easily — by making smart choices, instead of depriving yourself.

- Ditch old habits that don't serve you anymore.

- Finally, experience the changes you desire.

- Uncover more happiness, more energy, and a feeling of total balance throughout the day.

https://store.renewedlivinginc.com/secret-diet-free-gift-xyv248/?ref=27

Jill Jardine

Guided by the Stars and Soul

Everyone is born with gifts of intuition and soul wisdom. My life has allowed me to meet a wide range of people, whose different paths have taught me that the kind of life you have is connected to how you use that potential. Connecting fully with an awareness of my spiritual calling has enabled me to integrate my life experiences with many spiritual disciplines. I live with a sense of gratitude and purpose because I have come to understand that serving others is the key to personal freedom.

My most recent project, "Cosmic Scene with Jill Jardine," became recognized as one of international astrology's top 20 podcasts in under a year, when COVID forced me to find a new way to extend healing to a virtual audience. Years of training in dozens of healing modalities combined with impactful personal experiences (most notably four near-death experiences) provided the foundation for my podcast to deliver a message that resonated widely.

When I was younger, my path was not always clear to me because studying esoteric topics was not as common a few decades ago. One of the gifts that age brings is the understanding that different parts of your life fit together like a beautiful puzzle, once you commit to a path of service. Seemingly random interests inform a series of life experiences that shape your character to fulfill your destiny, if you have the courage to listen.

It might seem odd that a little blue-eyed blond girl from Connecticut would draw inspiration from Vedic practices in India, unless you consider one of my earliest memories. On a perfect summer day, I was making my way across a pool on a kickboard, when I lost my grip and slipped under the water. As I was drowning, I was not afraid but instead was drawn to a beautiful light and angelic voices and strangely familiar chanting.

While I was in a state of blissful reverie, my mother screamed for the lifeguard, who hauled me out of the water and resuscitated me. After returning to consciousness, I carried with me the understanding that it was not my time yet, along with a memory of Kirtan (Sanskrit mantra chanting). Following this experience, I had recurrent dreams about a previous life in India with vivid recollections of seeing my mother's body paraded to a funeral pyre. Fortunately, my mother is alive and well at the age of 89!

As a child, I experienced seeing things that others could not, particularly when traveling. My family explained that it was my active imagination when I was terrified by an apparition seeking my help on Long Island that my sister could not see. When living in New Zealand, visiting the Bay of Islands historic site, I observed a man dressed in Maori tribal dress that I pointed out to my brother who could not see him. I can still remember the Maori man jumping around laughing at me, who I later learned could have been a ghost of a Maori elder that those with "spiritual sight" sometimes see.

As an adult, I now recognize recurrent symbols in childhood dreams that I did not understand to be connected with Freemasonry and other esoterica. During my adolescence in the 1970s, I was drawn to tarot cards and astrology charts when "witchy" forms of divination were seen as residuals of the hippie movement. With the help of astrology books from a friend's mother, I gained enough knowledge to read charts and tarot cards for fellow high school students who were spooked by the accuracy of my predictions.

During my college days, I adored the new age bookstores in Harvard Square that provided something that my studies of Public Relations and Communications at Boston University could not. Since I enjoyed being part of the eighties' music scene in Boston, my continued interest in the esoteric studies led to my exposure to the Theosophical society, yogic philosophy,

Buddhist teachings, and Gurus.

I struggled to integrate my passion for understanding the esoteric world with a career in public relations, which led me to shifting my career focus toward teaching high school. My passion for the holistic life grew when I began doing yoga at a yoga ashram in Woodbury, CT, where I had the privilege of meeting the female guru Asha Ma, who had been initiated under Sri-Dyanyogi-ji before his death. This led to my experiencing a deep trance and receiving "Shakti-pat," which is a divine spiritual transmission from the guru.

This was a transformative experience that caused my past lives in India to flash before my eyes and led me to seek a Master's Degree in Counseling Psychology, where I studied Holistic Psychology and Jungian therapy. I was delighted to learn of Jung's deep appreciation of astrology. While pursuing my studies at Lesley University, I found myself back in Harvard Square working at Skylight Books, New Age Bookstore, and Harvard Law School. Let's face it, Harvard Law School wasn't the place for a spiritual girl to work. I transitioned into a job working for the Chair of the Harvard Anthropology Department.

Then my life took a mystical turn. In astrology, a major milestone is reached when Saturn returns to its birth position in your chart (typically at 28-30 years). Facing soul and family karma sets many of us up for big changes in direction. For me, this manifested one evening in Harvard Square when hearing "Inca Sun." The mystical sounds of the pan pipes caused me to go into a deep trance state, where an inner voice said, "If you turn around, your life will be changed forever." When I turned around, I met my first husband and father of my son Alexi.

My second near-death experience occurred when I gave birth to my son at Boston's Brigham and Woman's Hospital. My soul left my body when I was in labor, and my temperature reached 104 degrees due to a septic infection of my amniotic fluid. When I was floating above my body, feeling no pain, I heard, "Go back. The baby needs you to be his mother," which snapped me back into my body with a thump as all the pain rushed back in. I thanked God profusely for setting it up for me to go through this complicated birth in perhaps the best hospital in the country. I attribute my survival partly to the spiritual discipline of chanting the Gayatri mantra in the year leading up to Alexi's birth. The spiritual discipline connected to chanting Sanskrit mantras has both informed my spiritual understanding and offered continued protection during two more near-death experiences that occurred in the subsequent decade.

The next time I was sent back to my body was the result of a moped accident in Bermuda that left me unconscious for approximately 15 minutes, and a visitation from the Divine Mother who told me I would be fine because it was not my time. My fourth experience involved having my car demolished like an accordion by a drunk driver. Bystanders could not believe I escaped with minor injuries, but I knew I had been chanting Sanskrit mantras, so my survival made sense to me!

I share these deeply personal Near-Death Experiences because they have given me spiritual insight into the reality of spiritual protection and the power of the soul. Because of this, I have cultivated my spiritual understanding and incorporated it into my work as a counseling therapist, so that I may share it to help others heal. It's been a blessing to discover different talents and gifts developed in other lifetimes that help me in my work today. I had always had a sense that there is more to life than our physical existence and that we are guided by divine beings towards a higher reality, if we access them.

With this higher reality in mind, my spiritual development accelerated after the birth of my son. This included pursuing training and certification in three levels of Reiki (which at the time was still relatively unknown), homeopathic medicine, Acupressure, Shiatsu massage, alchemical breath work, vibrational healing, and mediumship.

I eventually quit my day job at Harvard University after connecting with my second husband. I opened a counseling and therapeutic practice to work as a healer incorporating all the various healing modalities I had learned.

This allowed me to counsel clients while offering healing sessions, facilitating hypnotherapy, doing psychic readings, and occasionally doing mediumistic work, where I could bring clients' loved ones through from Spirit.

I would be remiss if I did not mention that much of the wisdom I have been able to access comes from teachers who have impacted my understanding deeply. The astrologer Barbara Hand Clow, a renowned author and publisher, was my teacher who allowed me to participate in her 9 Dimensions Activations. I studied Dick Sutphen's teaching around past lives and was certified as a Past Life Regression Therapist and Alchemical Hypnotherapist through David Quigley's Alchemy Institute.

My true guru and teacher is Namadeva Archarya, Thomas Ashley-Farrand, who is a leading authority on Sanskrit mantra in the western world. During the 2000s, my focus turned toward the ancient Vedic practices of India and I pursued studies connected to healing in particular. Courses at Kripalu and Omega Institute, as well as studies at Far Horizons in California helped me to deepen my understanding.

Concurrently, I taught workshops/classes in Yoga, Yoga philosophy, Sanskrit mantras, and astrology. Part of my calling to serve others is to pass along the knowledge I have been so privileged to receive. This exposure led to my being offered the opportunity to do a radio program with WATD (near Boston), where listeners could call in and receive on-air readings. This was a first-of-its-kind show, but the success of these readings has inspired many others to offer healing in a similar format.

My private healing practice on the south shore of Boston flourished over the next decade, as I added further certifications as a Kundalini Yoga instructor and in Vedic Astrology. This allowed me to spread the healing wisdom I had been fortunate enough to receive beyond one-on-one counseling sessions. My work as a hands-on healer and teacher continued until March of 2020, when the whole world stopped and stayed at home because of the COVID pandemic.

In October 2019, I was receiving precognitive messages from my spiritual guidance telling me that an "airborne bomb" was due to hit at the historic Pluto, Saturn, Jupiter conjunction in Capricorn in early 2020. I thought it was going to be a literal bomb that was aimed at New York. I told people that I saw planes grounded and kept hearing the phrase

"airborne bomb." No one paid much attention, but I canceled all my travel plans for early 2020 during late 2019. My guides were accurately predicting and precursing the pandemic of COVID-19, caused by the airborne coronavirus!

The pandemic really drove home the lesson that sometimes something bigger than your physical reality is going on, and life challenges are not meaningless suffering. They represent moments of change where we are guided in a new direction, which for me has been the podcast "Cosmic Scene with Jill Jardine."

My work has evolved to Zoom sessions to international clients, most recently for the Cryptocurrency Community, and limited in-person counseling sessions, readings, and hypnotherapy. I am honored and privileged to share the things I have learned with a much wider audience. Things have a way of happening exactly as they are meant to when you walk in the true freedom of a path of service. The more we help others, the more our own suffering is mitigated. It truly is better to give than to receive!

Jill Jardine

Jill Jardine, M.A. Counseling/Psychology, is an International Professional Astrologer, Psychic, Healer, Hypnotherapist, and Yogi based in the greater Boston area. Jill is the host of the international podcast "Cosmic Scene with Jill Jardine," which is a cutting-edge podcast that brings in a new paradigm in the consciousness-shifting movement. On "Cosmic Scene with Jill Jardine," Jill shares astrological information and psychic hits on current and upcoming events. Jill interviews guests who are healers, yogis, and thought leaders in the Consciousness movement, who will deliver insightful and inspiring information to her listeners.

Jill has been helping groups and individuals for over 30 years in awakening toward higher consciousness, finding their path and purpose in life (Dharma), and shifting toward self-realization to live more fulfilling lives. Jill has been a pioneer in the new paradigm of the self-actualization and yogic movement since the late 1980s, which now flourishes. Jill has educational degrees, including a B.S. in Communication/Public Relations from Boston University, a teaching degree, and a Master's degree in Counseling which has helped legitimize her more esoteric teachings before they became mainstream. She has worked in the trenches with clients combining the modalities of Astrological counseling, Jungian therapies, Alchemical Hypnotherapy, Vedic yogic teachings, Sanskrit mantra and sound therapies, and other healing modalities. Jill has been certified in 3 levels of Reiki, Homeopathy, Acupressure/Shiatsu, Alchemical Hypnotherapy, Vedic Astrology, and a certified yoga teacher and Kundalini yoga teacher. She has been certified as a Sanskrit Mantra instructor and initiated into esoteric Vedic teachings through the lineage of Namadeva Archarya (Thomas Ashley-Farrand) and Guru Rama Mata and Sat Guru Sant Keshavadas.

Jill Jardine

Cosmic Scene with Jill Jardine

P.O. Box 633

Hingham, MA 02043

781-204-9350

JillJar123@gmail.com

www.JillJardineAstrology.com

Healing With Sound to Create Abundance

The Gong is a very powerful tool for sound healing and raising your vibration. As a practitioner who has used Crystal bowls, Drumming, Rattle, and Tibetan ceremonial bowls to perform sound healing, I was searching for an even more powerful technique. I have found the gong to be a superior modality for vibrational upliftment.

Ancient tribes (Tibetan monks, master yogis, and Hindu healers) discovered that when they use consistent, rhythmic beats and sound, they can induce a heightened state of consciousness. Depending on the frequency being played, this can elicit particular hypnotic responses from the listener.

The Gong Meditation in this course will create a vibration to help your mind and body heal and transform. Listen while meditating or any time you need to release what no longer serves. Do not listen to this meditation while driving or operating machinery.

https://JillJardineAstrology.com/Online-Courses/Healing-With-Sound-to-Create-Abundance

Shanon Boos

Mindset Matters Most

Here I am, 50 years old. I have lived a wild life. Good and bad, I wouldn't change a thing. If I could count on my fingers how many times random people have told me that I should write a book, I literally think I would need to use my toes. I don't think that is a common phrase to say to someone, so with over a dozen experiences so far... maybe these people are on to something? We are about to find out.

With the topic of **Limitless Women**, I'd like to give you a quick synopsis of my life.

I Went From:

- Having a dysfunctional childhood

- Multiple parental divorces

- Abandonment and parental alienation from my biological father

- Being sexually abused multiple times by multiple people for over a decade (child and adult, family and not)

- Being a troubled teen: shoplifting, lying, skipping school, and drug experimenting

- Dropping out of high school too stubborn to do homework. I chose to get my GED and move on with life.

- Having an abortion and remembering every detail because the "twilight" drug they gave you didn't work for me.

- Running away with a carnival (seriously... I left with them for a year when they came to town) My parents changed the locks on their house afraid of what I would become.

- Marrying a truck driver and becoming a female OTR (over the road) truck driver (in a time when very few women were on the road).
    - I met prostitutes in the bathrooms of truck stops. I chatted while doing our makeup together, asking them questions about their lifestyle and how they got into that position.
    - Listening to the CB radio, advertise an offer for "company," then witnessed a *very* pregnant "lot lizard" (truck stop prostitute) knock on the rig door next to us and get invited inside.
- Getting divorced three devastating times (but… hey — the 4th time I got it right)
- Filing for bankruptcy
- Having two of my four husbands hooked on pornography
- Being abandoned and alone when I was seven months pregnant (my second husband cheated and left)
- A single parent with no child support coming in, with tax liens, and a father who was 100% uninvolved
- Having to joint parent with a disinterested step-dad
- Having power shut off and eating tuna fish sandwiches by candlelight in late fall / early winter. Also sleeping bundled with my child with only the "unsafe" warmth of a three-wick candle.
- Losing my career and nearly losing my house to foreclosure (it was days away from being auctioned off, when I was able to stop the process and save it).

To Being:

- A Christ-follower
- A wife

- A mother

- A step-mother

- A national achiever in the nation's largest bank

- Multiple trips/bonuses/trophy earner in multiple companies and industries

- Consistently in the top 10% of my sales team

- Earning a six-figure income

- Being self-employed with multiple businesses and streams of income

- Launching: an evangelism ministry, speaking, podcasting, and writing

- Being a *Limitless Woman*

Like the infomercials always say, "But wait, there's more…" Yes, there truly is so much more to my story. Unfortunately, there is not enough room here for all those details. However, in my short time here, I will give you some insight into what I experienced, how it affected me, and how to truly become an overcomer. Through this sneak peek, I hope to promote hope and provide tools to others, so they can overcome the same and similar circumstances. I hope to teach people to become positive thinkers and overcomers. First, we need to learn that there are *Mindsets* and *Attributes* that overcomers have:

Words have POWER. Victimhood is a CHOICE. Progress requires ACTION. Sometimes ACTION in any direction is what you need to keep from SINKING. Indecision is a DECISION. Attitude determines ALTITUDE. If you think you can or think you can't — you are RIGHT.

Years ago, I created my own personal mantra with words I heard in the early '90s at a hypnotist show in Las Vegas, NV (sadly, I do not remember his name) and my now second favorite scripture… Philippians 4:8 I highly suggest printing it and taping it to the inside of your bathroom mirror. Read it often.

It Goes Like This:

What you think about, you bring about.

What you focus on, you magnify.

So, focus on whatsoever is GOOD, TRUE, PURE, NOBLE or of GOOD REPORT. If there is anything PRAISEWORTHY, focus on these things.

You see, the Bible tells us that there is the power of life and death in our tongue (words).

Words Matter — whether spoken out loud or internally as thought — they set your course. (Physiologically, your mind constantly seeks to prove itself true.)

This is why I say whether you think you can or think you can't — you are correct.

"As a man thinks in his heart, so is he."

—Proverbs 23:7 KJV

I believe the "power" the Bible refers to as life and death stems from energy flowing from our words. God created the universe with a word. The Bible states that Jesus is the word of life. I believe creation and human life are marvelous and unimaginably beautiful, and complex things that we can barely fathom to understand. And they are ***All*** made up of energy and frequency. (Google — What happens to plants that have loving words versus hateful words spoken to them for a period of time.)

An example is that ***Everything Has Energy***. Science shows us that energy is the building block of all matter (physical living beings and inanimate objects alike). Einstein said, *"Everything is energy, and that's all there is to it. Match the frequency of the reality you want, and you cannot help but get that reality. It can be no other way... So we get stuck at lower levels of energy and forget we're these powerful positive forces of nature."*

Tony Robbins has helped people raise their vibration to such a degree that they can literally walk on burning hot coals and not be burned for decades (and yes, I have done just that and bought one of the coals to commemorate). You don't have to understand something for it to be true. I can disagree that gravity exists, but a book will still hit the ground hard every time it is dropped from a high place.

Now, I realize that all this frequency talk sounds non-biblical or hyper spiritualistic. However, as with most things, science eventually just confirms what the Bible has said for centuries. I feel this is why so many people are infatuated with the recent trend of "manifesting." They are using words of affirmation or good vibes to get what they want in life. They are using biblical principles without giving God credit. (Side note: Some pastors also take it to an extreme with "name it and claim it, blab it and grab it" type theology.) I believe God gives us the desires of our hearts, but He also influences those desires. Also, please bear in mind that these are principles, not absolutes. We are just talking about words directing the energy.

***I feel like I need to pause right here. I am not a biblical scholar. I am not ordained and do not want to get into the theology of different religions etc. I do not intend to add or subtract anything from the word of God. These are my opinions. I am more of a "spirit of the law," not the "letter of the law" gal anyway. Just know that Jesus Christ is my Lord and Savior. I hope He is yours as well, or I get to introduce you to Him.

I would like to get back to energy and focus. I believe the reason the Bible tells us to fix our thoughts on Him and/or Heavenly things and to focus on "whatsoever is good, true, pure, noble or of good report. If there is anything praiseworthy, focus on these things" is to bring us into alignment with His will for our lives.

Is it possible that focusing on God or the good, praiseworthy things could raise your vibration? Is it possible that saying these positive affirmations, draws our mind into finding a way to make it come true? (To the best of your physical capability… of course.)

What I know is that **Focus** matters. Where you put your focus is what gets magnified, and it is where the energy goes. An example: My ADHD son's psychologist taught me to use "Positive Practice" with him. Instead of focusing on what NOT to do (fussing at my son while he was in the baseball dugout, antagonizing all the other boys to stop poking, prodding, making obnoxious noises, etc.) I was instructed to tell him what TO do instead. "Keep your hands to yourself. Let's watch the game and see what we can learn. Let's cheer for your teammates." That resonated with me so much! It reminded me of when my son was in kindergarten. He went to a private school because I wanted him to have a Christian education. What I found was that they did not have any understanding or the proper resources to handle a child like mine. Any normal kindergarten teacher would focus on praising the kids at every opportunity. It would involve stickers, stamps, treats, and praise of all kinds. However, not this teacher. She chose the two-strike rule instead. The kids started their day with green, and when they disobeyed, they were moved to yellow, then red. When red, she sent a note home to the parent. Let's just say that my son was red more often than not. (This was with her instituting additional strikes only for him using rubber bands she moved from right wrist to the left before changing his color.) If she didn't use the rubber bands, she couldn't make it to lunch. When I showed up for my first parent-teacher conference, she explained how she was forced to add rubber bands just for my son. She then presented me with a printout of ADHD symptoms from webmd.com and asked me to have him "checked." I asked her, "Why?" since I wouldn't medicate him. My response of not wanting to medicate made her jaw literally drop open. As she gaped at me, her shoulders dropped, head tilted forward in resignation at the realization that she was doomed to deal with this child for a few more months *unmedicated.*

I explained that I felt she needed to focus on the positive, as the Bible teaches. This was a Christian school, after all. I begged her to praise him like a normal kindergarten teacher would. What gets attention gets repeated… *Good or Bad.* I also explained that when you are looking for the positive, you find it. When you are looking for the negative and keeping track of the negative, your brain is on hyper-alert. It is looking for the negative to change the color or move that rubber band. It was where she put her focus *And His.* He stayed in that private school, until I caved to the pressure and medicated him the following year. A couple of months later, they expelled him anyway. I was so angry because there was only one month left of the school year. I had told them I "open enrolled" him into a nearby school, instead of planning to stay at the Christian school for the next year. At that point, they gave up and kicked him out with only five weeks of school left for the year. This stirred up my own rejection issues and added to his. *It was heartbreaking.* That heartbreak was compounded two years later, when there was a glitch in the "open enrollment," and my chosen school district had the legal right to turn us away based on the IEP (Individualized Education Plan) that they themselves created for him. When I got the denial letter, I was fit to be tied and wanted to fight it all the way. However, I calmly decided that forcing them to "keep him" would not be what was best for him. (Even if I would "win," they would likely take their frustration out on him. What would that accomplish?) I, therefore, chose to trust that God would work it out for our good. And He did!

When my son was at a private school, he hated it. When he was at public school, it was tolerable. However, when he got rejected and was sent back to our actual school district (where he had spent one month at the end of first grade), he now had the best teacher ever and suddenly *Enjoyed* it. (Nice one, God — He is funny that way.) My willingness to let go of my expectations and trust God (now looking for the positive) allowed us to transition well. This is the secret to turning a negative into a positive with your attitude. God's word actually says, *"He works all things out for the good for those that love Him and are called according to His purpose."*

When working through your current daily or historical life experiences, your embracement of compassion and understanding is pivotal. Forgiveness is also key to you living a peace-filled, successful life. I do understand that sometimes the pain is so great you cannot fathom ever getting to a place of forgiveness.

I ask you to try anyway, for your own benefit. Forgiveness does not mean what they did was not wrong. They do not have to be remorseful or apologize. Forgiving is saying that you will no longer hold onto pain, hurt, and negative energy in your heart. (For me, it is trusting that my God is a good God and trusting His Justice and His Plan.)

I have a favorite saying, *"Holding a grudge is like drinking poison and waiting for the other person to die."* Drinking the poison of unforgiveness only hurts you. Why give them that power? Have you ever been mad at someone for a period of time and see them, and immediately get your dander up only to find out they didn't even know you were mad at them or that they hurt you?

Forgiveness is a choice you need to make for your own sake. You may even have to make that choice over and over again, until it becomes second nature. (Sometimes, you have to keep saying it until you believe it.) I had a season of singing the Chris Tomlin song, *Good Good Father*, over and over every day, until I believed it. I then did the same thing for my current husband to help him get through custody complications after a devastating divorce. I sang it to him over and over until he believed it.

Also, our **Free Will** is one of our greatest gifts. We choose to love, choose to accept, choose to submit to God, and find freedom in ways the unsaved just don't understand. Salvation is a **Choice**.

The same applies to **Loving** someone (think of your spouse, child, or family member). It is a choice that we make. There is a fantastic book called *Love Is a Choice: The Definitive Guide to Letting Go of Unhealthy Relationships* by Frank Minirth and Robert Hemfelt. I highly recommend it. Over the years, I've learned that controlling people often refer to themselves as perfectionist, OCD, anal-retentive, and Type-A. They often have childhood trauma or abuse. The tool they use to help overcome their anger, fear, and trauma is **Control**. Something bad happened to them that was outside of their control, so now they try to control anything they can. In my case, it was ordering my three colored pens and sticky pads on my desk to be constantly perfect or my Skittles sorted by color. Silly stuff.

Please learn to channel that need for control into **Healthy** things like choosing to be happy in spite of XYZ. It is necessary to choose to let go of offenses. Choose to love that person who isn't doing what you would like them to do. We can't control others, but we can control our reactions to them. The power of choice — **Free Will** — is a God-given right all people have, regardless of their circumstances. I may have physical restrictions placed on me, but I have the **Free Will** to decide my mindset about it. Philippians 4:11-13 talks about learning to be content in all things.

With that said, you need to realize or understand that "Hurt people, Hurt people." Healed people grow, share, overcome, move on, and love to help people. They get to be happy and productive, etc. There is a fictional Christian movie called *The Shack* that can really help people understand grace and the healing of soul wounds. (Sidenote: There is a lot of controversy around the movie and book in the Christian community because of the author's theology and the use of multiple characters playing the role of God, including a woman.) However, I say, see it for what it is — **Fiction**. The choice of characters to play God the Father, Jesus, and Holy Spirit were just meant to give the main character a physical person to speak with. He needed to forgive others and forgive himself, before he could be free from the prison of offense and depression he was living in.

My prayer for each person that reads this book is to grow in relationship with God. Allow the Holy Spirit to heal you inside and out. I pray that the tools presented here help you become **Limitless**.

Shanon Boos

Shanon's middle name is Resilience. From being a high school dropout to a six-figure earner and national achiever, she is limitless. She grew up through family dysfunction, including multiple divorces, alienation from her biological father, poverty, molestation, and teen pregnancy. A high school dropout faced with an unwanted pregnancy, her hard knocks weren't over yet. Before she found God, she went through another decade of poor decisions, unhealthy relationships with people, and money.

She found it easy to earn money with natural leadership skills and work ethic. However, managing her finances/emotions was the hard part. She wasn't raised with financial responsibility. Thankfully, she ended up in a bank job and learned the skills needed to really succeed.

She became financially self-sufficient as an author and business consultant with a team of agents. Shanon is launching an Evangelism Speaking Ministry centered around teaching believers to share their faith with permission using turtles as a tool.

If you are a believer that has traditionally been afraid to share your faith, the TOFP Movement is for you. As a person who did not believe for many years and resisted any "unwanted" efforts at evangelism. I want to encourage and empower believers to share their faith without fear — with permission. When done in love and with permission, the gospel is received without resistance.

Shanon Boos
W1959 Spring Prairie Road
Burlington, WI 53105
262-716-4983
Shanon.Boos@yahoo.com

Breakthrough Business Advisors LLC
www.BBA-WI.com

Turtle on a Fencepost Movement
www.TOFPMovement.com

Eugenie Ermis

Reclaim You by Cleaning Your Mirror

Life Changer! Transformer! Hero! Brain Organizer! These are descriptors that my clients use after working with me. Goodness! What a difference a clean, well-lit mirror can make! I am so thankful that I found the Windex to clean mine!

The Reflection in the Mirror

It was in 1971 when my mirror began becoming murky and dark. This is the year I was uprooted from my home in Fairfield, California, and unsuccessfully transplanted in my mother's hometown of Summerton, South Carolina. It was in Summerton that I became acquainted with discrimination based on race, socioeconomic status, and appearance. As I began experiencing the teasing of my peers, negative comments from the adults surrounding me, and bullying, my perception of myself as a young girl began to become distorted. I began to become withdrawn, shy, and at times, I felt like ending it all. At one point, I thought I had made a friend for life, only to discover that she thought that I wasn't "good enough." She had transferred to my school and then ostracized me, when discovering that I wasn't one of the cool kids. It broke my heart. I also learned during that time that your "friends" could be cruel. I remember being locked, for what seemed like hours in the attic. I had to walk home in high-top Converse tennis shoes, after they had held me down and tied them together. There was also the pain of being called "a leftover" by a peer whom I dearly loved and the extreme embarrassment of auditioning for cheerleader and not receiving a single vote. Later, a male peer informed me that it was because I was not pretty enough. Oh, and a comment that would always hurt me to the core came from a friend of mine's mother. She always found an occasion to comment on the fact that my youngest sister was beautiful. She would make a comment, "Your sister must have come from the milkman because she is so gorgeous!" This woman knew how to strike to the core.

The image I saw in the mirror became so murky and dark that I could not see myself anymore. I began wearing the masks of "the good little girl" and "false piety" to protect myself and establish a false identity. These masks protected me for decades. I was very tired of holding them up but even more terrified of letting them down. Who was I without them?!?

Jesus, the Windex for the Mirror

Decades passed, and I continued to hold up these masks. I felt invisible, unworthy, and sometimes suicidal. However, no one knew as long as I held up these masks. I would have thoughts such as, "No one would miss me if I were gone. Why do I stay?" The pattern was exhausting, and I longed to experience true friendships again.

In 1997, I found the Windex for my mirror. For the first time in my life, I experienced the genuine grace of God and knew I was loved for me-the real me. I experienced this grace through a Vio de Christo retreat and truly never looked back. You see, during this retreat, I was able to drop the masks and allow Jesus to heal the pain of broken relationships. When I looked into the mirror, I could both see and feel the love of Jesus staring back at me. Boy! What freedom this was! No more masks and knowing the authentic, genuine love of Jesus! Indescribable! Does this mean I have been on the easy street since that point?!? No way! However, I now have the confidence needed to walk through any storm to the other side. I see my authentic self and use my voice. I know that Jesus is always in my corner and always loves me! This has freed me to have authentic, genuine relationships with those around me. It has also helped me to recognize the people to keep in my life and those to let go.

Serving Others

I now serve 50+ Christian women in reclaiming their core self and authentic voice through the power of story, identifying patterns and the masks they have worn, and mirror work. I feel that it is my purpose to build up other women, so that we can improve our communities by using their voices and mentoring the young women and girls to follow.

Anne

Anne, beautiful Anne, couldn't look at herself in the mirror, without seeing her abusive Dad looking back at her with a face of condemnation and hate. She had carried the pattern of hurting before being hurt her whole life and wanted this pattern to stop. She didn't want to sabotage her current relationship and felt that she might. Through the use of story, mirror work, and timeline work, Anne was able to stand up to her Dad, rescue her terrified inner child, and enjoy a more authentic relationship with her husband and family. She is now living the "life of my dreams!" Best of all, she loves herself and knows that Jesus loves her unconditionally.

JoAnn

JoAnn, tough as nails JoAnn, was a marshmallow inside. She had worn her mask of "I don't care what you say about me" for many years. The wearing of this mask was costing her dearly. She was losing the relationship with her children, her business was faltering, and she also found her health deteriorating. JoAnn had allowed the perceptions and abuse of her alcoholic husband to totally wound and skew the reflection she saw in the mirror. Through finding patterns in her story and mirror work, JoAnn now loves herself, has terrific relationships with her family, and her business is thriving again. She was also able to set firm boundaries with her now ex-husband and realizes that she is good enough on her own. She is worthy and valuable.

Stevie

Stevie, a very kind and loving woman, had a very cluttered home and mind, which was causing her tremendous stress and anxiety. She literally was attempting to hide herself behind the multiple layers of clutter to protect herself from ever being hurt again. She also felt that if people could see the "real" her, they wouldn't like her. Oh, and heaven forbid, they ever find out about her past. Stevie began to see how living this cluttered life was beginning to take a toll on her relationship with her family, and she struggled to concentrate at work. There was more stress at home, which led to increased stress at work. The pattern was exhausting! Through the use of story and re-framing, Stevie was able to slice through the clutter of her mind and soul. She was able to forgive herself for past "mistakes" and was also able to forgive her family members for their betrayal.

Now when Stevie looks into her cleaned mirror, she sees a beautiful, capable, strong woman who is not only a better administrator (she got a promotion!) but is able to have an authentic, loving relationship with her husband and child.

Conclusion

Life Changer! Transformer! Hero! I have done all the hard work to claim these descriptors and shorten your journey in finding your authentic life and voice! Allow me to help you, so that you can see **your** reflection clearly in **your** mirror!

I help 50+ Christian women find their voice and reclaim their core self, so that they can experience more fulfilling and mutually beneficial relationships and live their best life now.

Eugenie Ermis

Eugenie is a middle-aged woman who has definitely learned how to clean her mirror. She continually works to remove any smudges that appear. She has also learned to love herself warts and all, which can sometimes be a huge project.

Her thirty-eight years of experience as a registered nurse, mainly in the behavioral health arena, has taught her invaluable active listening skills and the ability to recognize patterns in ones' story. Because of her uncanny ability to read between the lines, you may think she is a mind reader.

Eugenie is a certified Transformational Coach through the Health Coach Institute and The John Maxwell Team. It is through this training that she developed her primary modality of using story and mirror work in helping women heal and transform.

Eugenie is an avid nature lover. She lives in Manning, South Carolina, with her critter crew. On warm, clear nights, you can find her walking at night listening to nature's symphony.

Eugenie Ermis, RN, CTC
Awaken Your Roar Transformational Coaching
1758 Kenwood Road
Manning, SC 29102
803-460-7429
https://AwakenYourRoar.us

---

45 Minute Transformational Coaching Session

In this coaching session, you will be able to:

1. Identify at least one limiting pattern in your life.

2. Identify at least one action step to create a new affirming pattern.

3. Learn the basic Mirror Exercise.

https://AwakenYourRoar.us

Jenny Lundquist

Newfound Wings

I hear the school bell ringing loudly, echoing through the long white hallway. I take a deep breath, smile, and step into my high school 1st-period class. I am thrilled to be there! I feel refreshed after just having had an amazing basketball practice earlier that morning. I can feel myself getting stronger, my skills improving, overall becoming a better player. My coaches are seeing it too! They are giving me more playing time in games. I am going to become a starter. That's the goal. I reflect on when I first came to this school, and I am thankful that I went outside my comfort zone and joined the team as an outsider and a newbie! Everything was going great!

Then, Bam!

It was only a few practices later when I took an incapacitating hit to my head. I was hurt bad, and just like that, I lost everything. In a single moment, the thing I enjoyed most vanished. I couldn't play anymore, my friends slowly faded away, and my sacrifices started to seem pointless. The rest of high school was a blur. I don't remember being angry or sad, or scared. All feelings just disappeared. I became consumed with numbness, empty, like a seashell that lost its pearl.

The thing about a brain in pain is that no one can see it. There is no visible wound, so people can't empathize. People who have gone through a brain injury themselves can understand, to an extent. It still affects everyone a little differently. There are some standard repercussions to getting hit in the head: sensitivity to noise and light, loss of balance, loss of memory, and sometimes even loss of happiness. However, for me, cognitive function didn't compare to the most significant loss that I experienced. I had studied neuroplasticity. I understood that the human brain could rebuild itself. A person can repair neural pathways and do exercises to help reorganize their brain structure.

What I COULD NOT FIX, NO MATTER HOW HARD I TRIED, was my identity.

I used to be a student-athlete. I have always been a hyperactive person. I came out of the womb a few weeks early. By nine months old, I was walking. Within 12 months, I started climbing. They had to move me out of the infant room in daycare and put me with the two and three-year-olds. When I was three, you could find me zooming down the sidewalk on a bicycle. Yes, I did have training wheels, but they were more for show than support. They didn't actually touch the ground. You see, little me would take corners so fast that it bent up the arms to those extra wheels. To cope with my hyperactive and dare-devilish nature, I became an athlete. Being an athlete allowed me to continue to push my limits and burn through my energy in a healthy way. **I was an athlete.**

When I was ten years old, I started doing mixed martial arts. MMA gave me a place to train hard, both physically and mentally. I built physical strength, flexibility, balance, and techniques to defend myself. In addition, I learned respect, perseverance, humility, integrity, leadership, and other essential life skills. My participation in martial arts lasted for six years. Throughout those years, I was able to earn a second-degree black belt. I competed in tournaments, breaking boards, sparring, grappling, and showing my skills with weapons and self-defense techniques. I was also on a demonstration team and a leadership team, where I taught some classes. I absolutely loved it! Along with doing martial arts, I took part in a few other sports. **I was an athlete.**

In middle school, I tried a variety of team sports. I played softball for a month. I played intramural football, and I played ultimate frisbee. I tried track and even volleyball. Unfortunately, none of these sports gave me what I needed. They all limited the athletic potential I knew I had. I knew I wanted to do something extremely physically and mentally demanding, that I could continue doing throughout my school career. Ultimately, my team sport of choice was one where you could hear the squeaky shoes on a gym floor and see a big orange ball fly through the air. **I was an athlete.**

Basketball was fun for me. I wasn't that good when I first started playing, but it checked most of my boxes. It was important to me to play a sport in school because it was my way of contributing and belonging to a community. It also held me accountable for my grades. So, I started playing when I was in the 7th grade. Wanting to become a better player, I started watching a lot of basketball videos from high-level coaches. Eventually, I even started learning about sports psychology.

When I started high school, I made a callous decision to stop doing martial arts. If you know anything about high school sports, you know it requires an extreme time commitment. A part of me also knew that if I wanted to become great, I needed to dedicate myself fully to training and learning the game. Martial arts had been a major part of my life and personal development. It had also been a coping mechanism. The relationships that I had developed with the people I trained with were like no other. Eventually, I decided to let go and fully immersed myself in the life of a high school basketball player. I loved belonging to the circle of athletes. I also loved the challenge, but I couldn't have possibly begun to fathom how challenging things would get.

One of the biggest challenges I faced was pushing through injuries. People describe me as a tough cookie. I am strong. I have determination, a winning mindset, and a highly competitive drive. However, as competitive as I am, I also respect rules. I was the type of athlete who always played hard but never dirty. No matter the day, I would give 110% of myself out on the court. I was a team player. I developed the footwork to be a top defender. I learned how to score and was able to get rebounds. These skills made me dangerous, and it made others mad.

My tiny body accumulated an upsetting number of injuries, by taking elbows and getting tripped and pushed around. I realized how violent girls' basketball could be and how aggressive girls could get. The competitiveness turned dirty. We lost count of the bruises, scratches, and times that I rolled an ankle. I snapped a bone in my wrist, had a near torn ligament in my knee, and took a few blows to the head. Wack! That was it. The last hit to my head took me out for good. After that, everything went dark, as if someone flicked a light switch. **I was no longer an athlete.**

At the time of my last concussion, I was a junior. That year I had been a high-performing athlete and student. I had worked my way up to play on the varsity team. I was also taking honors and college-level classes. I had worked my butt off to get my spot and play in games for this team. After the last hit to my head, I lost all that I had worked for, I felt that my sacrifices were meaningless, and honestly, I lost myself. Doctors and my parents told me that I couldn't play anymore or even return to martial arts. I lost the relationships I built with my teammates and other high school athletes. I was no longer one of them, so they didn't care about me. I lost my motivation to do well in my classes. I started to hate going to school. I didn't know who I was anymore. This injury forced a change in my path.

For months, I was sucked down deep into a very dark hole. The repercussions of my severe concussion limited me. I couldn't go to school. I couldn't learn. I couldn't do any exercise, and I couldn't do any of the things I enjoyed doing. I was suffering. No one truly knew how much pain I was in and how close I was to giving up. I call it my hibernation, except I'm not the type of person that's meant to hibernate.

I finally made a decision. I told myself that I would get better. I told myself that I could redefine myself. I refused to be limited by stupid high school stereotypes. I had to say to myself I was going to be okay, even though I wasn't one of them anymore. I was no longer an athlete.

Sitting on the floor in my dark bedroom with my back against my closet door and my fan blowing cool air, I pulled out my phone. I opened my YouTube app. I started watching videos. Searching for motivation, I came across videos from experienced and wise professionals like Denzel Washington, Tony Robbins, Joe Rogan, and many others. I slowly began to pull myself back together. With newfound motivation, I was able to battle through the negative thoughts. During my healing process, I had a lot of time for deep introspective thinking.

Born with an innate gift for awareness and the trained awareness I learned from martial arts, I became hyper-self-aware. Understanding myself and my thoughts, I was eager to pull myself out of the abyss. However, I didn't know where to start. I began to dive deeper into psychology to understand better how my brain worked and ways that I could heal it. As I read online, I discovered the terms that described precisely how I was thinking, feeling, and acting. The more I read, the more I also began to understand others. I learned about what led them to their decisions, and what influenced their actions. My eyes became drawn to seeing how the world affects the human psyche.

At this point, I was still trying to redefine myself. I needed to figure out who I was without being an athlete. I felt wrapped up in a small cocoon. However, I was desperate to get out and stretch out my newfound wings. These things just take time, I guess.

Patiently waiting, the last semester of my senior year in high school rolled around. My English teacher assigned a video project. The project was to create a memoir in video form. The main focus was on individuality. It involved answering what makes an individual unique and the individual you are. Of course, this is the big question I thought. Little did I know how big of a gift it was. It forced me to reflect on myself even more.

The answer that I formulated and the truths I discovered while working on this project are as follows:

- To be an individual, you must not be afraid to be vulnerable.

- Lean into your true self. Don't let stereotypes limit you.

- There are sacrifices to embracing your uniqueness, but your happiness is worth it.

- An individual is the sum of ALL of their life experiences.

- Growth is inevitable and things change. However, you are in control of how you grow.

- Stay kind and help others when you can.

I clearly remember when my final video was played on the giant white smart board that hung in the front of the classroom. It was the last video to be played. I could feel my stomach drop and the cold hard surface of my desk in front of me. I had laid my head down, wanting to disappear.

The teacher hit the play button, and my classmates began to watch and hear me explain the realizations I made while trying to redefine myself. Finally, I worked up enough courage to look up from my desk and look around that classroom full of my classmates. Everyone had their eyes glued on that screen, and nobody was moving. You literally would have been able to hear a pin drop. I was amazed at how captivating the video I created was to a room full of high school seniors on their last day of school. I remember the roaring cheers and comments of amazement and inspiration sparked from my video.

From this experience, I learned a few more lessons:

- Sharing your unique story can help someone else.

- You never know what someone else might be going through. You never know how big of a positive impact you can make on them.

- I also realized how powerful videos could be.

Over time, I noticed the rising popularity of video content on social media and how technology has evolved to allow people to share video content easily. Videos saved me, and I used videos to save others. I now help businesses create videos to save their audience.

My mission is to help speakers, educators, and entrepreneurs share their stories and lessons through impactful video media to attract attention from their audience.

I help create engaging video assets for businesses, by incorporating psychology, video editing, and social media. Videos can be an extremely effective marketing tool. Through visual and audio cues, you can build deeper connections with your target market and spark inspiration.

I now work online with people from all over, helping them create videos that take their businesses to the next level. As a video editor and content educator, I can make various videos for you to use to share your stories and expertise.

Check out my free resources at JenRoseMedia.com to see tips on how to create powerful videos and how to strategically share video content on various social media platforms.

Jenny Lundquist

Jenny Lundquist is a badass intuitive. She is notorious for pushing limits and inspiring those around her to do the same. At a young age, Jenny was exposed to the world of entrepreneurship, by following her mom around to business conferences. As life went on, Jenny stuffed away her entrepreneurial spirit. She got an internship in high school and decided to go to college. While going to school, she had a great opportunity to work as an engineer in a manufacturing plant. Three years later, she was left feeling limited, powerless, and not herself. It was as if she were another cog in the wheel. With her whole life ahead of her, she wanted to lean into her true self and desired to make a difference in the world.

She finally let loose her entrepreneurial spirit and embraced her creative side. Jenny paired her passion for creating videos with her interest in psychology and founded Jen Rose Media. She helps speakers, coaches, and small businesses gain attention and inspire their target market through powerful and engaging videos. Jenny strategically creates high-converting video content using subtle marketing techniques backed by psychological studies. We live in an impersonal world, but consumers crave deeper connections to the brands they invest in. Jenny's mission is to ensure that her clients are heard and seen above their competition and help them build connections with their future clients.

When Jenny is not working, you will likely find her outside enjoying the fresh air on two wheels. She enjoys riding her motorcycle on the backroads between Illinois and Wisconsin. Jenny also likes to ride her dirt bike off-road, racing down trails, or hitting jumps on a motocross track. At home, she loves to relax with a cup of coffee cuddled up next to her dog.

Jenny Lundquist
Jen Rose Media
Illinois
JenRoseMedia@gmail.com
JenRoseMedia.com

A Simple Guide for Creating a Video

Are you filming on your own as a business owner? This short guide will walk you through the basics of creating a video to use in your business. Get some ideas on what and how you can start recording today, right now.

https://JenRoseMedia.com/my-gift

Each episode features today's top influencers and entrepreneurs on the rise as they share empowering stories and ninja tips meant to become the

FUEL TO IGNITE
a positive change in your life.

bit.ly/ompclr

YOUR STORY

Harness the Power of Story
to Build Your Brand & Attract Clients.

FREE GIFT

Learn how your story can position you
uniquely in the marketplace,
attract clients, and distinguish yourself
from all competition.

OvercomingMediocrity.org/Freebie

Made in the USA
Columbia, SC
10 October 2023

24215771R00152